T0374245

ELLERY H. HUNTER

The Second Peter Principle

Keys to Becoming an Effective Christian

authorHOUSE®

AuthorHouse™
1663 Liberty Drive
Bloomington, IN 47403
www.authorhouse.com
Phone: 1 (800) 839-8640

Scripture taken from the NEW AMERICAN STANDARD BIBLE®, Copyright © 1960,1962,1 963,1968,1971,1972,1973,1975,1977,1995 by The Lockman Foundation. Used by permission.

THE HOLY BIBLE, NEW INTERNATIONAL VERSION®, NIV® Copyright © 1973, 1978, 1984, 2011 by Biblica, Inc.® Used by permission. All rights reserved worldwide.

Published by AuthorHouse 03/13/2017

ISBN: 978-1-5246-7207-2 (sc)
ISBN: 978-1-5246-7205-8 (hc)
ISBN: 978-1-5246-7206-5 (e)

Library of Congress Control Number: 2017902618

Print information available on the last page.

Any people depicted in stock imagery provided by Thinkstock are models, and such images are being used for illustrative purposes only. Certain stock imagery © Thinkstock.

Author Photograph: Images by Marc Anthony

This book is printed on acid-free paper.

CONTENTS

DEDICATION

This book is dedicated to my children, Christopher, Ashley, Andrea (Andi) and Adrian (Micki). You all are my greatest accomplishment. I'm proud of each of you. My hope is that the key ideas in this book are not new to you. My prayer is that you will take these and teach them, by word and example, to my grandchildren. (Aaron, Cato, Xavier, Amari, Caleb, and Mackenzie…)

WITH GRATITUDE

My deepest gratitude is owed to my Lord and Savior Jesus Christ and your Holy Spirit for guiding, empowering, and inspiring me to share what you have given me. To my wife Nina, your love is my constant stimulus. Thanks for all the encouragement. To my mom, Mother Louella Hunter, the example of a Godly life and your devotion to His Word has been a guiding light – thanks Mama. Thanks also to a couple of brothers in Christ who have encouraged and even pushed me to do this. Terry Moss, we've had many great conversations, but none as powerful as the night you challenged me by asking, "So why haven't you finished the book?" Thanks, my friend. Johnny Crockett, now you can quit asking, "when is the book coming out?" every time I see you. Thanks for encouraging me, and for waiting. And also, thanks to all the folks at Authorhouse Publishing for all your expertise.

PREFACE

Like anyone else, I have dreams and aspirations. I admire people who have accomplished great things, and I hope to one day be considered one of them. I want to make an impact on others—to make a difference. But my dreams are not always so altruistic. I also dream about enjoying the finer things in life. On my drive to work, I often imagine myself behind the wheel of the luxury car in the next lane. When I arrive home at night, I secretly long to see the Publisher's Clearing House Prize Patrol van pulling in behind me to deliver my huge check. In my spare time, I like to meticulously plan what I would do with the millions of dollars in cash I would receive. I have even written it down—careful to deduct tithes and taxes off the top. You wouldn't believe what a generous, honorable person I would be.

While I'm waiting on the magical to happen, I've decided to be practical. I can't claim to have come up with this perspective on my own, though. The Bible has a way of bringing me back to reality. In His famous sermon recorded by Matthew, Jesus Christ uttered the memorable words, "But seek first His kingdom and His righteousness; and all these things shall be added to you" (Matthew 6:33).

This book is about being practical. I firmly believe that God has placed in our hearts the desire to be great—we are made in His image. I also am convinced that, for a variety of reasons, greatness escapes many of us. Some of us settle for being superficial—we just try to look great. Some people attempt to closely duplicate another person's greatness—failing to realize their own unique gifts. And some people mistakenly believe that, because they don't have a talent that the world idolizes, they can't be great. This last thought is particularly faulty because it shows a complete misunderstanding of what really defines greatness. True greatness is being like God.

But even knowledge of that fact can be misapplied. Individuals who were trying the wrong way to be like God have made the biggest mistakes in history. Adam and Eve ate the forbidden fruit because Satan tricked them into thinking that doing so would make them like God (Genesis 3:5). Satan himself was evicted from heaven because he attempted to make himself like God and rule heaven (Isaiah14:14). However, the Bible tells us that we can and should be like God—in our characters. We should think and behave like Christ (Phil 2:5).

The point of writing this book is to explain something that I did not learn until well into my adulthood. Specifically, I wanted to crystallize this for my children and grandchildren, who presumably have lots of time ahead of them to use it. The principle and accompanying qualities that I am writing about are universal and powerful. They are useful. And most importantly, they are biblical.

INTRODUCTION

I've been a Christian for over twenty years now. I wish I could say that I've been a great Christian for all this time, but the best I can say is that I've been an intentional Christian. By that, I mean that I have always tried to figure out how to be a great Christian. At one time, I thought being a great Christian meant being so righteous that no one could honestly say that I had sinned since my conversion. It didn't take long for me to blow that one. I've tried at various times to be a great Bible scholar (not smart enough), a great preacher (not charismatic enough), a great church leader (not visionary enough), and a great pastor/shepherd (not patient enough). After much inner turmoil and disappointment, I finally realized that trying to be a great Christian is like putting the proverbial cart before the horse. First, I have to figure out how to be an effective Christian. In a sense, when I stopped trying to be a great Christian in other people's eyes, I think I became a better Christian. Here's how.

The Bible teaches us what we need to know about God and His plan for this world. Through it, we receive knowledge about the origins of mankind, the history of the people that God called his own, the Jews, and about the origins of Christianity. But more importantly, the Bible teaches us how to live a productive and Godly life—today. By studying the Bible, we can discover timeless principles about how the world works and how to live according to those principles. But let's face it—most of us don't want to become Bible scholars. We just want to know, in a nutshell, what we need to know in order to live a productive, blessed life.

Fortunately, there are certain passages of scriptures that summarize principles that are practical and universal. One such passage is 2 Peter 1:3–11.

> His divine power has given us everything we need for a godly life through our knowledge of him who called us by his own glory and goodness. Through these he has given us his very great and precious promises, so that through them you may participate in the divine nature, having escaped the corruption in the world caused by evil desires.

> For this very reason, make every effort to add to your faith goodness; and to goodness, knowledge; and to knowledge, self-control; and to self-control, perseverance; and to perseverance, godliness; and to godliness, mutual affection; and to mutual affection, love. For if you possess these qualities in increasing measure, they will keep you from being ineffective and unproductive in your knowledge of our Lord Jesus Christ. But whoever does not have them is

nearsighted and blind, forgetting that they have been cleansed from their past sins.

Therefore, my brothers and sisters, make every effort to confirm your calling and election. For if you do these things, you will never stumble, and you will receive a rich welcome into the eternal kingdom of our Lord and Savior Jesus Christ (NIV).

This is from the second letter written by Peter to first century Christians. Peter was one of Jesus' closest disciples and considered one of the leaders of the early church. In this passage, Peter reveals a principle that is the key to our Christian life. In summary, he explains that God guarantees that, if we develop Christ-like character, we will be effective and productive in all that we do. I call this **the Second Peter Principle**. The gist of this principle is taken from verses 3, 4, 8, and 10. In verse 3, Peter says that God has given us everything we need for our natural and spiritual life through our knowledge of Christ. In verse 4, he explains that God promises that we can take on the nature of God. In verse 8, he promises that if we grow in certain characteristics, we will be effective and productive. And in verse 10, Peter emphasizes the promise by saying that if we follow this, we will never fail. So, God has given us everything we need to be effective and productive, by growing in characteristics that are exemplified by Christ. In most of the other verses, Peter lists the characteristics or qualities that make up a Christ-like character. The qualities are interrelated, and together make up a system that supports the Second Peter Principle.

There are a couple of aspects of this principle that are particularly interesting—it is universal, and it is guaranteed. The Second Peter Principle is universal in the sense that we all have the capacity to develop and exhibit these qualities that make up Christ-like character. They aren't given to only a select few, fortunate people. These qualities aren't reserved for the super-anointed, or highly talented. We all have these qualities in some portion, and we all have the ability to develop them further.

The Second Peter Principle is also universal in the sense that it applies to both our spiritual and natural lives. The New American Standard Bible translates verse 3 as "His divine power has granted to us everything pertaining to life and godliness." That means we can apply this principle to any good goal and it will work. For example, if a person wants to be a doctor, they can apply this principle to becoming a doctor and it will work. In the following chapters, I will particularly highlight this aspect of the qualities. Of course, the real purpose for the system is plainly described by Peter. The point is to "become partakers of the divine nature." (2 Peter 1: 4) The highest use of this system is to become like Christ, that is the goal of every Christian.

Peter also makes a bold statement that makes this one of the most powerful passages of scripture. Peter says that this system of qualities is accompanied by a promise from God. God, through His word, has promised that if we live by this system we will never stumble, and we will be effective and productive in our Christian lives. If you believe that God keeps His promises, you have to pay really close attention to what Peter says here. God *guarantees* that if you live by this system you will be effective and productive in your life.

So, over the next few chapters we will explore these qualities that make up a systematic way of life and form the backbone of the Second Peter Principle. This system, if followed, will make us effective, productive Christians. Along the way, we will also point out the universal application of these qualities, as well as what the Bible and others have to say on the subject.

CHAPTER 1

DILIGENCE—"BE ABOUT IT"

"If you wanna be somebody, you wanna go somewhere, you better wake up and pay attention." This is a memorable line from the movie *Sister Act 2*. It was delivered by Whoopi Goldberg as Sister Mary Clarence, a Vegas lounge singer turned fake Catholic nun/high school music teacher. She's addressing her hooligan inner-city students, who all just happen to have enormous musical talent. In the movie, the class turns her off-the-cuff admonishment into a catchy pop tune. The hook in this movie is that this improbable group of teenagers—led by their even more improbable teacher—actually wakes up and pays attention, wins a choir competition, and saves their school. The story illustrates how, if you harness your talent and apply yourself, you can overcome circumstances and be successful. The students, though talented, appeared to be going nowhere until Sister Mary Clarence gets them to pay attention to their gifts and apply themselves. They set a goal—winning the choir competition—practice, and overcome obstacles to reach success. They worked diligently to win the competition.

1

Over the years that I've spent working on this book, I've had to deal with a couple of things that made it difficult to complete. Aside from the fact that I'd never written a book before, the main complication has been the amount of time that it took. I'd been thinking about this book for a long time, but actually sitting down and putting this all into words has been more than a notion. Because of that, the process has been marked by starts, stops, and restarts. It seems like once I got a little momentum, life sidetracked me. Though I intended to get right back to it, I would go weeks without writing a word. It usually took deliberate planning and a conscientious effort to resume this project. But because you are reading this, you know that, ultimately, I completed what I started.

The quality that I had to put into practice in my own life and in the process of writing this book is the first principle that Peter mentions in this system: diligence.

In 2 Peter 1:5, he instructs us to "make every effort to add to your faith." In other translations, the phrase "make every effort" is substituted with the phrase "applying all diligence." Diligence means to give attention and care to something. In a legal sense, we speak of "due diligence," which means the attention and care that is required. So to be diligent means to maintain attention to something to make sure you are doing what is necessary. Sister Mary Clarence implored her students to wake up and pay attention. Where I'm from, we had a phrase that encouraged people to be diligent about pursuing their expressed plans. "Don't talk about it. Be about it."

In the book of Romans, Paul states that diligence is the critical quality for exercising leadership (Romans 12:8). He says leaders should govern "diligently." This gives a good illustration of what diligence means. In a sense, it also means to be serious about something. If you are going to do it, then you have to be serious about it! You have to be about it! Imagine a leader of an organization or government who lacks diligence. He or she would fail to give attention to the organization, and before long, there would be a noticeable decline in the effectiveness of that organization. If the leader is "asleep at the wheel," as the saying goes, then people under him or her would likely become lax in their responsibilities as well. The same is true of governing ourselves. If we are not diligent in managing our own lives, we become lax in the responsibilities we have. Perhaps this is what Solomon meant when he said, "Keep your heart with all diligence, for out of it spring the issues of life" (Proverbs 4:23).

Jesus Christ displayed just how diligent and serious He was at the age of twelve. Luke tells a story of His family's annual trip to Jerusalem for the Passover feast. When the rest of the family left to return home, young Jesus stayed behind in the temple, listening to the discussions, asking questions, and answering questions from the Jewish teachers. He was there for four days before His family returned for Him. When they finally found Him, his mother asked Him why He'd caused them such anxiety. His response was "I must be about my Father's business" (Luke 2: 49, KJV). Although we are tempted to think that Jesus had all knowledge and wisdom at birth, this shows that He was diligent about learning and preparing for His later ministry. Scripture supports this view in verse 52. "And Jesus kept increasing in wisdom and stature, and in favor with God and men." When it came to ministry, Jesus showed early on that He was going to be about it.

Peter lists diligence first of the principles, but he doesn't exactly say it's part of the list. Instead, he says, "apply all diligence" to cultivating these qualities. Diligence is necessary to make the system work. The reason that's true is because we have a tendency to get distracted, especially when it comes to doing something that takes a long time. Often it is easier to do things that can be completed in one sitting, but if we have to drop it and pick it up again later, it is more difficult to finish. For example, there are lots of people who have yet to earn a college degree that they started years ago. Once you get out of the swing of going to class and doing homework, it's hard to get back into it again. It's like that with most things that require multiple efforts. Once you stop doing it, it's harder to get going again. So to complete a difficult undertaking, you have to get serious and be about it.

Thinking of diligence as being serious about something also highlights its necessity. We really only maintain the effort and focus on something over an extended period of time if we are serious about it. I can't count the number of things that I started doing on a whim, only to conclude fairly quickly that I'm not really that serious about it. For example, because I love music, I have always dreamed of playing an instrument. In junior high school, I played the bass horn, which most people call a tuba. I was pretty good at it too. But since playing the tuba wasn't considered cool, I stopped playing in high school. Nevertheless, my interest in playing an instrument hasn't waned. As an adult, I have actually purchased a keyboard, a full drum set, and not long ago, I talked my kids into buying me a guitar for Christmas. Unfortunately, I still can't actually play any of them. The truth is I was never serious about learning to play any of those instruments.

So for something this important, Peter wanted to make sure to start by saying we must be diligent; we must be serious about developing these qualities and maintaining focus. If you are going to pursue becoming like Christ, you have to "be about it!"

In fact, if you want to accomplish anything that is worth accomplishing, you'd better "be about it!" Diligence is one of the qualities that has a fairly obvious universal application. Unfortunately, it is also one that too many of us neglect. Most of us desire to accomplish something great. Few people set out to be average. But often the difference between merely dreaming and actually realizing our dreams is diligence. Being great requires more than talent; it requires diligence. Malcolm Gladwell illustrates this in his 2008 book, *Outliers*.

In his book, Gladwell discusses some fascinating theories about what extraordinary achievement can be attributed to. He cites studies of experts and top performers in areas like computer science, basketball, and fiction writing to understand what they have in common. Gladwell reports that one of the key factors is that those who have become experts at something have typically practiced their craft much more than others. He notes,

> The idea that excellence at performing a complex task requires a critical minimum level of practice surfaces again and again in studies of expertise. In fact, researchers have settled on what they believe is the magic number for true expertise: ten thousand hours.[1]

That's ten thousand hours of practice at a specific skill. When you consider all of the other things we have to do in life—like sleep and work—ten thousand hours spent on one thing is an awful lot of time. According to Gladwell, Bill Gates started computer programming in the eighth grade. Over the next few years, he and some friends spent an enormous amount of time programming. They borrowed time on mainframe computers in the evenings and on weekends. In the summer, they spent as much as eight hours a day, seven days a week, on it. By the time he was a senior in high school, he had convinced his school to let him spend the entire spring semester on an independent study program writing computer code for a local company. When he dropped out of Harvard to start Microsoft, he had spent well over ten thousand hours practicing his craft.

This is characteristic of those we consider geniuses. It is said that Leonardo da Vinci, who is widely considered one of the greatest painters of all time—and was the creator of the *Mona Lisa*—once drew a human hand one thousand times in an effort to perfect it. Think about the stories of young athletes pounding a basketball for hours at a time and then becoming an NBA player. Or consider the young musician who spends all her spare time playing her instrument and then growing up to be a musical genius. It takes more than just talent to be great at something. It also takes the diligence to actually do it, day after day, week after week, and year after year. You have to *be about it*! Whether you want to be a doctor, an NBA player, or a writer, you have to get serious and apply yourself—you have to *be about it*!

Food for Thought

And we desire that each one of you show the same *diligence* so as to realize the full assurance of hope until the end.

—Hebrews 6:11

But without faith *it is* impossible to please *Him,* for he who comes to God must believe that He is, and *that* He is a rewarder of those who *diligently* seek Him.

—Hebrews 11:6

He who diligently seeks good seeks favor.

—Proverbs 11:27, NASB

Only give heed to yourself and *keep your soul diligently,* so that you do not forget the things which your eyes have seen and they do not depart from your heart all the days of your life; but make them known to your sons and your grandsons.

—Deuteronomy 4:9

Lazy hands make for poverty, but diligent hands bring wealth. He who gathers crops in summer is a prudent son, but he who sleeps during harvest is a disgraceful son.

-Proverbs 10:4-5, NIV

If a man is called to be a street-sweeper, he should sweep streets even as Michelangelo painted, or Beethoven composed music, or Shakespeare wrote poetry. He should sweep streets so well that all the hosts of heaven and earth will pause to say, "Here lived a great street-sweeper who did his job well."

—Martin Luther King Jr.

The leading rule for a man of every calling is diligence; never put off until tomorrow what you can do today.

—Abraham Lincoln

CHAPTER 2

FAITH—"YOU MUST BELIEVE"

In the spring of 1963, the Southern Christian Leadership Conference (SCLC) began an organized campaign of demonstrations and boycotts designed to break the stranglehold of racial discrimination in the city of Birmingham, Alabama. Led by the local chapter's leader, Rev. Fred Shuttlesworth, and national president Rev. Dr. Martin Luther King Jr., SCLC was attempting to strike a mortal wound to the discriminatory system called Jim Crow by protesting in what was then considered the most segregated city in America. The direct but nonviolent protests were meant to pressure the city government and local businesses to the negotiation table as well as bring media attention to the plight of black Americans in Birmingham. SCLC and Dr. King had been successful leading nonviolent protests and a bus boycott in Montgomery, Alabama. However, they had failed to make significant gains in subsequent campaigns in Albany, Georgia, in 1961 and 1962. Furthermore, sit-ins and freedom rides led by the Student Nonviolent Coordinating Committee (SNCC) were achieving some success, while Dr. King's profile was losing some luster. The SCLC and Dr. King were in a watershed moment in 1963. The government leaders in Albany, Georgia, had been successful against the protest movement by using legal maneuvers, as well as painting Dr. King and SCLC as outsiders who were bent on upsetting what they considered their genteel way of life.

It was then that Dr. King and SCLC trained their sights on Birmingham and their blatantly racist Police Commissioner, Eugene "Bull" Connor. However, the protesters met with much the same tactics in Birmingham as they had in Albany. The city leaders responded with clever tactics of their own. They obtained a court injunction to stop the marches, making them illegal. As they arrested the protesters by the hundreds, they also sought to cut off their financial lifelines by refusing to accept bonds from the bail bondsman used by SCLC, claiming that he did not have the requisite assets to cover bail for so many people. When Dr. King and other senior leaders of the movement chose to buoy the spirits of the protesters by physically joining the marches, they did so with little confidence that they would be able to make bail. Thus, on April 12, 1963, Dr. King was arrested in Birmingham, Alabama, and was immediately put into solitary confinement. He would later write of the fear and despair he felt in that dark cell, unable to even get word to his pregnant wife, Coretta, that he was okay.

But one of the hardest blows Dr. King would receive in that Birmingham jail cell would come when someone slipped him a copy of the next day's newspaper. In it he read a full-page ad, signed by a group of influential Birmingham clergymen, opposing the marches. In their letter, "A Call for Unity," these clergymen commended the government for its calm handling of the demonstrations, which they deemed both unwise and untimely. Further, they openly implied that the SCLC tactics incited hatred and violence. In essence, some of his brothers in the gospel (as well as a rabbi) accused Dr. King of causing violence and hatred. In response, using the margins of the same newspaper, Dr. King wrote what came to be published as his "Letter from Birmingham Jail." In the letter, Dr. King brilliantly laid out the case for why the demonstrations were necessary and refuted every argument leveled at him using perfect logic, reasoned counter arguments, and powerful illustrations. And to completely dismiss his religious detractors, Dr. King was crystal clear in explaining why, in the face of such insidious opposition, he pressed on. He wrote, "If the inexpressible cruelties of slavery could not stop us, the opposition we now face will surely fail. We will win our freedom because the sacred heritage of our nation and the eternal will of God are embodied in our echoing demands."[2] Dr. King overcame because he believed he would. He believed that victory was inevitable. He overcame because he had faith.

As Christians, our goal of becoming like Christ begins with faith. We strive to be like Christ because we believe in Him. But an important question is—what do we believe about Him? Let's look at it another way. If you consider the story of Jesus of Nazareth and just look on the surface, you may not find a lot of reasons to imitate Him. Here are some of the facts. He was a Hebrew carpenter who lived a couple thousand years ago in Palestine, which, at the time, was under Roman occupation. He lived a relatively short life on earth and, during the few years He did live, He seemed to have a death wish. He never married and had no children. He quit his job to roam around the countryside where, even though He helped lots of people and even performed miracles, at the end of His life he had very little to show for it. He apparently had no house of His own—He stayed with relatives and friends. His preaching caused the religious officials to charge Him with blasphemy against God, and He was ultimately executed at the age of thirty-three with only a handful of relatives and friends at His side. They couldn't even afford to purchase a tomb to bury Him.

Why do we want to be like Christ? Remember: Peter identifies our goal as seeking to "participate in the divine nature." The only reason to want to imitate Jesus Christ is because you have faith—you believe Him to be God and you depend upon His death as payment for your sin. Just based on the earthly record of His life, we might find reason to look elsewhere for a role model. But if you agree to pursue the promises that God has given, "so that through them you may participate in the divine nature," then you do so because of faith in Jesus Christ. You do so because you believe that there is more to Him than just the facts I mentioned above. You want to become like Christ because of your faith that He is the Son of God and Savior of the world. It must begin there.

The writer of Hebrews famously wrote, "Now faith is the substance of things hoped for; the evidence of things not seen" (Hebrews 11:1, KJV). As poetic as this verse sounds, it doesn't really get to the practical definition of faith. To uncover the definition of faith we must look at the context of Hebrews 11:1. This letter, written to the Hebrews, is an eloquent sermon. It was written to a group of

Jewish believers who had endured persecution and suffering because of their association with Christ. The writer reminds them that Christ is superior to the Jewish laws and traditions of their heritage. These new Christians of Jewish heritage had lost family and property because of their newfound faith. These believers were being urged to maintain their confidence that they would receive what God has promised since they had "done the will of God" (Hebrews 10:35–39). Considering this, we can see that faith is not merely mental belief, but it is belief that has reached such conviction that we rely upon the object of our faith. It means to believe something (or in someone) to such a degree that you act accordingly. Dr. King didn't just sit at home believing that black Americans would gain their civil rights— he believed it so much, he acted upon it.

The simplest metaphor I've heard for the definition of faith involves a belief that a chair is sturdy enough to hold you. You may declare your belief in the capacity of the chair to keep your butt from hitting the ground. However, this declaration is not true faith until you actually sit in the chair with your full weight. In Hebrews 11, faith is illustrated by citing several biblical characters that exhibited faith. In each case, the resulting action of those cited was the key factor. By faith, Abel offered, Enoch pleased, Noah built, Abraham obeyed, and so on. A critical, defining characteristic of their faith was the fact that they acted it out. James was much more direct with this point when he wrote, "For just as the body without the spirit is dead, so also faith without works is dead" (James 2:26).

Interestingly, in Peter's letter, he doesn't list faith as a quality to be obtained—he assumes that we have it. This makes perfect sense when you consider what we are doing. Peter is prescribing these qualities, which will make us like our Savior, Jesus Christ. Through these, we will become "partakers of the divine nature." Of course, before we can even begin to become like Christ, we must first actually believe in Him and trust that He is someone worth imitating. Jesus Christ is our Savior and Lord. Furthermore, he is the example of a human who lived in perfect harmony with the creator. He was sinless. If we don't believe in Jesus Christ, and desire to become like him, then we may not even attempt to develop some of these qualities. Therefore, Peter is writing "to those who have received a faith of the same kind as ours" (2 Peter 1:1).

One of the most important ways that faith is exercised is through prayer. No one prays to a God that they don't believe exists—that would be insane. But those of us who believe in God pray to Him because we believe that He hears us and that He will help us. We pray to God because we believe that He is able to do what we ask—whether our request is for simple guidance or for deliverance during an urgent crisis. It would be foolish to pray to a god who you don't believe exists. Likewise, it wouldn't make sense to pray to a divine being who we don't think cares about us and our plight, or to a deity who doesn't have the power to help. Just as we lean on Christ for our salvation, we pray to God to help our family, our friends, our nation, and ourselves. We pray because we have faith.

It is rather apparent that in order to accomplish anything, we must have some degree of belief that we can do it. In fact, it is not likely that we will even make an honest attempt to do something that we do not believe we can do. It would be a waste of time and energy. Are you really going to borrow well over a hundred thousand dollars in loans and devote four or five years of your life to go to medical school if you don't really believe you can be a doctor? I don't think so.

Please note, however, I am not here advocating faith as a magical, mystical power that will bring to you whatever you are believing for. I am not suggesting that you can simply believe your way into prosperity, effectiveness, or anything else. As I mentioned before, faith is to believe in something or someone to the point of acting accordingly. If you believe you can be a doctor, and you actually want to be a doctor, then you will study hard, go to college, and go to medical school. That's faith. Believing you can be a doctor but doing nothing to become a doctor is not faith. That's wishing—as in, "I wish I could be a doctor." Believing you can be a doctor but not applying yourself in school is hoping. Faith is critical to achieving anything, but it is still just one of the qualities.

Food for Thought

But without faith it is impossible to please Him, for he who comes to God must believe that He is, and that He is a rewarder of those who diligently seek Him.

—Hebrews 11:6

Faith is to believe what we do not see, and the reward of faith is to see what we believe.

—Augustine

For they conquer who believe they can.

—Virgil

For whatever is born of God overcomes the world; and this is the victory that has overcome the world— our faith.

—1 John 5:4

Therefore, having been justified by faith, we have peace with God through our Lord Jesus Christ.

—Romans 5:1

Every man lives by faith, the non-believer as well as the saint; the one by faith in natural laws, and the other by faith in God.

—A. W. Tozer

Faith is deliberate confidence in the character of God, whose ways you cannot understand at the time.

—Oswald Chambers

Faith means trusting in advance what will only make sense in reverse.

—Philip Yancey

Chapter 3

MORAL EXCELLENCE / VIRTUE— "DO THE RIGHT THING"

The third quality that Peter encourages us to add is moral excellence, or, in the King James Version, virtue. In a way, the lead character in Spike Lee's movie *Do the Right Thing* illustrates it negatively. Once you get past the excessive profanity in the movie, you see that it is about a young man living in difficult circumstances. He has not always done what is right, but he is trying. His surroundings, the Bed-Stuy section of Brooklyn in New York City on an oppressively hot day, seem almost like hell. His baby mama is an annoying young lady who can make the hair on your neck stand up when she says his name—Mookie. Although he's not very good at it, Mookie is trying to do what he thinks is the right thing. He's trying to be a working man, delivering pizzas for Sal's Pizzeria. But the police kill his friend, Radio Raheem, because Raheem refused to turn his boom box volume down inside Sal's. Even when Mookie throws a garbage can through Sal's window to incite a riot, he thinks he's doing the right thing. He is reacting to bad things going on around him. In fact, everyone *thinks* they are doing the right thing—Sal, by staying in the neighborhood, the cops by protecting Sal, Radio Raheem by refusing to mute the Public Enemy track that represents his attitude toward life, and the neighborhood instigator, Bugging Out, by asking Sal, "How come ain't no brothers on the wall?" Sadly, this behavior is what passes for virtue in our society. According to this film, "do the right thing" means do what is right for *you*. And that illustrates why virtue is an unpopular concept. Real virtue is hard to find.

The word *virtue* is an old-fashioned but interesting term. Today, some may use it as a euphemism to refer to a woman's reputation—as in, "a woman must protect her virtue." It is a word that is used in the Bible only a few times, and modern Bible translators have replaced it with the term *goodness* (NIV) or *excellence* (NASB). Of the four times it is used in the New Testament, three of the times it was used by Peter. In the above passage in second Peter, I think the term *virtue* fits best. It means moral uprightness. If I were writing a dictionary, I'd probably define it as the desire to do the right thing.

In a world driven by selfish behavior, true virtue is something that is hard to find. It requires that you look beyond yourself to determine what is right. In other words, virtue is not what's right for *me*, but what God says is right. Many people go through life and allow the circumstances around them to dictate their behavior because they are chiefly concerned with what they need to do to have a successful, or comfortable, or secure life. They react to what's going on based on what they need to do to protect their own interests. In this world, most people live like Mookie. Virtue has no place in a world filled with this mentality. The movie illustrates that you cannot look to popular culture to find the definition of virtue or morality. Though everyone in the movie thinks they are doing the right thing, the combination of their actions produces a riot. But if you look hard enough you can find real virtue. It usually follows faith. When we come to faith in the supreme God, we need to change that old way of thinking. Doing the right thing means doing things the right way—God's way.

Additionally, there is something interesting about this quality that we notice when looking at its use in the Bible. *Virtue* or *excellence*, when they are used to refer to man, mean doing the right thing, or doing things the right way. In the classic Greek world of the New Testament, it carried the connotation of being honorable. It was the quality expected of a leading man of the day. However, in the Bible, it is also used to refer to a tangible quality Jesus Christ possessed. In fact, in Luke 6:19[3] and Luke 8:46,[4] virtue is said to have emanated from Jesus when people touched him, and it caused them to be healed. One of those references is the familiar story of an unnamed woman who had been suffering from hemorrhaging for twelve years. She secretly touched Jesus' coattail, and was healed. Jesus, however, noticed what happened and described it as, "Somebody hath touched me: for I perceive that *virtue* is gone out of me" (Luke 8:46, KJV, emphasis mine). More modern translations substitute the word *virtue* for the term *power*. So, in its purest form, *virtue* or *excellence* contains power to set things right!

For those of us who are Christians, this additional understanding points out why virtue is necessary. When we exhibit virtue—when we do the right thing—it has an impact on the environment around us. Perhaps you've been in a situation where people were acting in ways that were wrong, but when someone stepped up and did the right thing, others began to follow them. Oftentimes, there are people around you who are simply doing wrong because it's what they see everyone else doing. But when a virtuous person comes around and does what is right, it gives others permission to do what they know they should. This won't work on everyone—some folks are going to do wrong no matter what. But there are usually some people who are just waiting on someone else to do the right thing. I can't emphasize this enough. Too often, we assume that we will be at a disadvantage somehow if we do the right thing. We think that others who are not burdened by the desire to do what's right will take advantage of us. However, we fail to consider that when we do what is right, we change the atmosphere. Our virtue, like Jesus', has power.

Another, more fundamental, explanation for its necessity has to do with the work of God. God created the world in which we live. Furthermore, He created this world to work a certain way. He designed extremely complex systems that make the world work. Consider the complexity of the human body (obviously created by God). We have systems like the respiratory system, circulatory system, and nervous system, that all work together in a delicate balance to keep us alive and allow us to think, move, breath, and everything else. But when we do things with our bodies that are not consistent with God's design, things go bad—we get sick, we lose functionality, we may even die. Likewise, when we live in ways that are inconsistent with how God designed the world, things don't work the way they should. Real virtue—doing the right thing—is necessary because it means we are doing things consistent with how the world really works.

The universal application of virtue is captured well by Steven Covey in his popular book, *The 7 Habits of Highly Effective People.* Covey encourages his readers to adopt the habit of beginning an endeavor, "with a clear understanding of your destination." He furthers explains this habit by writing, "it means to know where you're going so that you better understand where you are now, and so that the steps you take are always *in the right direction.*"[5] Even if you take this out of the moral/religious context, there is a right way to do anything. The right way is the way that will produce the desired result. But we often take another way because of convenience or distraction. When we lose focus on our goals, it is easy to get off the path that leads to the fulfillment of those goals. In general, doing the right thing means doing the things that lead to where you are trying to go.

But let me be blunt—it is foolish to think of what is right without considering the moral context. To do so is to discount your own values. Covey is not simply writing about accomplishing goals—he is writing about becoming the person you want to be. You may technically become a doctor by getting a medical degree, but if you cheat on tests, purchase term papers, and bribe professors, you will have taken the wrong road. Furthermore, eventually these wrong actions will be uncovered—perhaps when you get sued for malpractice. Honoring moral principles such as honesty allows you to live with a clear conscience and without fear of being found out.

It is critical that, no matter what we are trying to accomplish, we remember not only to do it the right way, but also to do the right thing.

Food for Thought

Finally, brethren, whatever is true, whatever is honorable, whatever is right, whatever is pure, whatever is lovely, whatever is of good repute, if there is any excellence and if anything worthy of praise, dwell on these things.

—Philippians 4:8, NASB

Virtue is to the soul what health is to the body.

—François, Duc de La Rochefoucauld

The virtue of a man ought to be measured, not by his extraordinary exertions, but by his everyday conduct.

—Blaise Pascal

Do all the good you can, to all the people you can, in all the ways you can, as often as ever you can, as long as you can.

—Charles Haddon Spurgeon

The good man is his own friend.

—Sophocles

Then the Lord said to Cain, "Why are you angry? And why has your countenance fallen? If you do well, will not *your countenance* be lifted up? And if you do not do well, sin is crouching at the door; and its desire is for you, but you must master it."

—Genesis 4:6–7

CHAPTER 4

KNOWLEDGE—"GET AN UNDERSTANDING"

You've probably heard the saying, "It's not *what* you know. It's *who* you know." I personally think that both are important. But, I heard a great story not long ago that illustrates the importance of *what* you know.

There was a young man in high school named Johnny who'd been born with only one arm. With only his right arm, this young man could still lead a relatively normal life and do most things— however, the one thing he wanted to do was to be a wrestler. He tried to join the wrestling team at his high school but was cut. Johnny was determined, so he sought the help of a retired wrestling coach in town. The old man agreed to tutor him on the condition that Johnny practice with him every day and do exactly as he said. The teen agreed and reported for his workout the next day. The old coach spent an hour teaching the young man one wrestling move and then had him run two miles. The following day the coach had him practice the same move and then had him run two miles again. Each day for a month they did the same routine with the same move.

Just as Johnny was starting to wonder if it was worth all the trouble, the coach suddenly announced that he'd arranged for him to compete in the regional wrestling tournament that would feature some of the best wrestlers in the state. Having only learned one move, Johnny was filled with self-doubt. "Do you think I can win?" Johnny asked.

The old man nodded and said, "I believe you can."

Johnny didn't even tell his parents that he was competing because he was afraid that it would be a disaster. His first match was against a younger foe who appeared to be even more afraid than Johnny. Within thirty seconds, Johnny pinned the young man and won the match. He did the same with his next opponent and moved to the semifinals. Though he'd won two matches, Johnny was concerned now because the remaining wrestlers were more experienced than the last.

Before stepping on the mat, Johnny looked up at his coach and asked, "Do you think I can win?"

The old coach nodded and said, "I believe you can." Johnny won the next two matches by pinning his opponents.

But when they announced whom Johnny would meet in the final match, he shuddered with fear. The final opponent was a two-time state-champion wrestler. Though they were the same age, the other teen looked to be five years older. What was more frightening was that this wrestler had a reputation for not only beating his opponents, but also inflicting as much pain as he could.

Before he walked toward the mat, Johnny turned to his coach and asked, "Do you really think can I win this one?"

The coach looked confidently at Johnny and said, "I know you can."

With that, Johnny stepped on the mat and began to wrestle. It was a tough match, and Johnny avoided being pinned for two minutes. Finally, he saw an opening. Johnny made his move. Everyone stood to their feet and applauded as Johnny pinned the two-time state champion.

After they'd hung the champion's medal around Johnny's neck and he'd accepted the congratulations of all the other participants, Johnny headed to the locker room. When he got there, he had just one question for his coach. "How did you know I could win? I only knew one move."

The coach smiled and said, "You only needed one move. The move I taught you could only be countered by pulling on your left arm."

The young wrestler knew only one move. His coach knew that his one move could not be countered. Sometimes what you know makes all the difference.

Peter tells us to add knowledge to our virtue and our faith. Defining knowledge is simple—it's acquiring knowledge that is complicated. This is especially true when we are talking about knowledge of God and His word. But an important clue is provided by the words Peter chooses to use in his letter. The term that Peter chose to use in this passage means general knowledge—the type gained through observation and experience. He's referring to knowledge gained, not only through reading or listening to someone else, but knowledge gained by experience. It is a practical, useful knowledge that Peter is encouraging us to obtain. And the way to obtain it is to hear what God has said (the Bible) and understand it by applying it to your life.

Let's take the concept a bit further. Often, the Bible talks about knowledge as part of a package that includes two other terms—*understanding* and *wisdom*. In Proverbs 2:3–6, Solomon wrote, "For the LORD gives *wisdom*; From His mouth come *knowledge* and *understanding*" (NASB). In general, to know something is "to perceive directly with the mind or senses."[6] To understand something means "to perceive and comprehend the nature and significance of it."[7] And to have wisdom is to have an "understanding of what is true, right, or lasting."[8] Taken together, Proverbs tells us that God gives us the ability to perceive things directly through our senses, to comprehend the significance and nature of things, and to use it all to determine what is true and right.

Let me begin the discussion of why knowledge is necessary by going back to the main idea of this book. God has given us everything we need to live as he intended for us to live. His intention is that we would become like Christ, which is to say, to live as effective and productive Christians.

With that in mind, what if we don't know what it means to become like Christ? What happens when we have an erroneous understanding of what being a Christian means? I think this is a huge issue in some circles today. Peter says we have been given everything we need, "through the true knowledge of Him who called us by His own glory and excellence." In other words, what we need is available to us who have true knowledge and understanding of God. We have what we need to the degree that we know and do what God says.

The Apostle John tells of a series of a conversations Jesus had with some of the religious officials of his day. At one point Jesus convinces some of them to believe in Him and tells them, "If you abide in My word, then you are truly disciples of Mine; and you shall know the truth, and truth shall set you free" (John 8:31–32). This statement points to an interesting concept. If the truth sets you free, then error or ignorance binds you. This is what happens when we have an inaccurate understanding of God's word—we are bound.

For example, when we believe that Jesus was rich and that God intends for all of us to be rich, we start pursuing riches. Not only do we pursue it but we are also restricted from hearing what God says about the subject. This is because, generally speaking, once we form a certain belief, we tend to subconsciously interpret new information in a way that is consistent with our existing belief. By the way, Paul says, "But those who want to get rich fall into temptation and a snare and many foolish and harmful desires which plunge men into ruin and destruction" (1 Timothy 6:9). The point is, misunderstanding God's word regarding the pursuit of riches leads us to ruin.

Peter explains that the cultivation of these qualities, including knowledge, is part of the process of knowing Christ. He says, "For if these qualities are yours and are increasing, they render you neither useless nor unfruitful in the true knowledge of our Lord Jesus Christ" (2 Peter 1:8). The knowledge he is referring to includes experience. In order to truly know Christ, we must apply His word to our lives. As we do, we experience a deeper understanding of His ways and how they work.

Knowledge is universally recognized as foundational to the human experience, especially in our contemporary world. However, it has been popular in some circles to question the real value of education—especially a college education. With the cost of college rising to seemingly ridiculous sums, some people wonder if it's worth it. This notion is compounded by the anti-intellectual strain that can be found in some communities. It is not uncommon for young students who do well in school to be teased by their peers. Being called a "nerd" or "lame" is hard to take for junior high or high school kids. But make no mistake about it—knowledge is power! And the more knowledge you have, the better equipped you are to do most anything.

Let me be more specific. According to a report by the College Board, "there is a correlation between higher levels of education and higher earnings for all racial/ethnic groups and for both men and women.[9] ... Over their working lives, typical college graduates earn about 73 percent more than typical high school graduates, and those with advanced degrees earn two-to-three times as much as high school graduates."[10] The report points out that studies have shown myriad personal and societal benefits to achieving higher education.

Of course someone will say, "I know a lot of people with degrees who have been downsized from their jobs." That is probably true, but it doesn't erase the value of education. Per the College Board report, a college graduate is still less likely to be unemployed than a high school graduate. And more importantly, in the economy of the present and future, the value of knowledge is becoming even more important. For example, author and *New York Times* columnist

Thomas Friedman interviewed a corporate executive who admitted to being "a job killer." The executive, who had led several technology companies, stated that he was in the business of killing jobs by replacing them with technology. When asked what jobs could *not* be killed, he offered that those who'd learned to be creative at what they did and who provided unique value, like subject-matter experts, were most valuable.[11] He added, "But the days where people could assume [that] if they worked hard and the company they worked for was successful, [this] made them 'safe,' is now over."[12]

Increasingly, the difference between living comfortably and being in poverty is education. And while it is true that there are some people who have a college degree but are poor, even those people have a greater chance to escape poverty. But it is not the piece of paper that is important—it is what you learn. In achieving a college degree, you sharpen your writing, reading, and thinking skills. In earning a degree, you show others that you can complete a complex task while overcoming plenty of obstacles. And as the fictitious one-armed wrestler can attest, sometimes just one bit of knowledge can be exactly what you need to reach your goal.

Food for Thought

Acquire wisdom! Acquire understanding! Do not forget nor turn away from the words of my mouth. Do not forsake her, and she will guard you; Love her, and she will watch over you. The beginning of wisdom is: Acquire wisdom; And with all your acquiring, get understanding. Prize her, and she will exalt you; She will honor you if you embrace her.

—Proverbs 4:5–8, NASB

For if you cry for discernment, lift your voice for understanding; If you seek her as silver And search for her as for hidden treasures; Then you will discern the fear of the LORD And discover the knowledge of God. For the LORD gives wisdom; From His mouth come knowledge and understanding.

—Proverbs 2:3–6, NASB

Buy truth, and do not sell it. Get wisdom and instruction and understanding.

—Proverbs 23:23, NASB

He who asks a question is a fool for five minutes; he who does not ask a question remains a fool forever.

—Chinese Proverb

The more that you read, the more things you will know. The more that you learn, the more places you'll go.

—Dr. Seuss

You can never have a Christian mind without reading the Scriptures regularly, because you cannot be profoundly influenced by that which you do not know."[13]

—R. Kent Hughes

Chapter 5

SELF-CONTROL—
"CONTROL YOURSELF!"

The first chapter of the book of Daniel introduces us to a young Jewish man that would become one of the heroes of the Bible. We've all probably heard the story of Daniel in the lion's den. But chapter 1 tells how Daniel got to be the king's top advisor. Daniel was one of the Jews who was enslaved by King Nebuchadnezzar and taken back to Babylon.

The King decided to start a training program for young men to become his personal assistants. He took the best and brightest from among the slaves and ordered them to be educated and groomed for his service. Young Daniel was among those chosen for this plumb opportunity. The program included giving them treatment that ordinary slaves, and even regular citizens, would envy. They were provided the best food and drink, including wine.

The King wanted his potential assistants to know how to handle themselves in a palace environment and look good doing it. The problem was that the king's diet plan, though sumptuous, was prohibited by Jewish law. Apparently, most of the chosen Jewish slaves jumped at the chance to be part of the program and eat the delicacies required. But Daniel and three of his friends were determined to resist. They did not want to defile themselves by eating and drinking what the king required.

So, Daniel and his three friends proposed that they be allowed to eat only kosher food and abstain from wine. They were willing to be judged against the others who ate the gourmet meals. This part of the story ends with Daniel and his three friends, Shadrach, Meshach, and Abed-Nego becoming the top students in the program and the healthiest.

Daniel and his three friends perfectly illustrate the quality of self-control. They were faced with a choice between following their convictions about what God had said and following the crowd to do things that seemed pretty enjoyable. I imagine they did consider going along with the program, since, after all, it meant they would eat tasty food and drink great wine. If someone told me that in order to qualify for a better job I had to eat at the Cheesecake Factory every day, I'd ask if this was a dream. But Daniel gambled that God's way was better in the end, even if it meant refusing to do something that nearly everyone else found enjoyable. He and his friends exercised self-control by continuing to turn down the king's gourmet meals.

With the Second Peter Principle, Peter is communicating the details of a program that leads to us becoming effective and productive Christians. And the next quality that we are to cultivate as part of this program is self-control.

Self-control is easy to understand but very hard to do. What's worse, it is something that a part of each one of us is opposed to. In a way, we do not want to control ourselves—we want to be free. We want to do what makes us feel good. We want to enjoy the things that are enjoyable—to the fullest. And the things we don't want to do, we don't want to do them. But self-control means doing things that we don't want to do but that we know are good for us. It also means refraining from doing the things we know are not good for us, even though we really want to do them.

In particular, self-control means controlling not just our actions, but also our passions, impulses, emotions, and even thoughts. There is a saying whose author is unknown that goes, "Watch your thoughts; they become words. Watch your words; they become actions. Watch your actions, they become habits. Watch your habits, they become character. Watch your character; it becomes your destiny." While I certainly can't disagree with this, every time I hear it, or read it, I think about how hard the first two points are. Even the Bible affirms how difficult it is to control our words when James writes, "No one can tame the tongue, it is a restless evil" (James 3:8). But the wisdom of this is evident. My parents will attest that I could have avoided a lot of trouble growing up if I had learned to keep my mouth shut.

To this point we've looked at self-control from a negative perspective. But self-control is important for very positive reasons. If we can exhibit a measure of control over ourselves, we will be better able to summon the will to do what we need to do when things get harder. This is best exemplified regarding athletics. The Apostle Paul uses this logic in his first letter to the Corinthians, using a runner as his model. He notes that athletes exercise temperance and moderation in all things so that they can win the race. He has in view the notion that a runner must discipline himself through training and keeping his body in top condition in preparation for the race. I am no runner, but even I know that you won't win many races if you don't train and treat your body right.

In terms of being an effective and productive Christian, self-control is required because of the very real opposition we have to this goal. Once we become Christians, we take on the nature of God through His Spirit that comes to dwell within us. However, we still retain our human nature (the flesh). Our flesh is not inclined to do what God wants of us, while our mind, having accepted that we are Christians, wants to follow God. This sets off the internal war that we experience daily.

The apostle Paul describes this battle in Romans. He says, "I find then the principle that evil is present in me, the one who wants to do good. For I joyfully concur with the law of God in the inner man, but I see a different law in the members of my body, waging war against the law of my mind and making me a prisoner of the law of sin which is in my members" (Romans 7:21–23, NASB). So, prevailing in this battle requires controlling our flesh. To the degree that we can do that, we are able to do what God wants us to do. Like the runner, we have now trained, and we are ready to do what we need to do.

The obvious challenge with self-control is learning how to do it. While I don't have the space to give an in-depth answer, there is a key that I can provide. In reality, self-control is a somewhat deceiving term. Although we must make the attempt to control our flesh, we cannot do it alone.

Once again, it's the apostle Paul to the rescue. In his letter to the Galatians, he gives a list of qualities that are produced by the Holy Spirit, who comes to dwell in us and help us. He says, "But the fruit of the Spirit is love, joy, peace, patience, kindness, goodness, faithfulness, gentleness, self-control" (Galatians 5:22–23, NASB). So Paul confirms what we have learned from Peter—we already have what we need for life and godliness. We have the Holy Spirit within us, who produces self-control, among other qualities. *It is incumbent upon us, not so much to generate self-control, but to yield to the Holy Spirit within us, who produces self-control.*

Going back to his letter to the Romans, Paul explains that the key to winning the battle between the flesh and the Spirit is our mind. Specifically, he says, "For those who are according to the flesh set their minds on the things of the flesh, but those who are according to the Spirit, the things of the Spirit" (Romans 8:5, NASB). If we are consistently thinking about what we want and what we enjoy, we have our minds on the flesh. But the more we think about what God is doing and what God wants, the more we will have our minds on the things of the Spirit.

This also applies to what we put in our minds via television, reading, and even conversations. If we are constantly feeding our minds with fleshly things, it will be much harder to control our flesh. This is why viewing pornography is so harmful. Viewing images of naked people is likely to make it harder to control one's lust (no pun intended).

Another personal example of this involves my appetite for desserts. I really need to limit how many sweets I consume. It's a much harder battle to win if I'm having dinner at The Cheesecake Factory. Looking at the large, well-lit display case full of sumptuous desserts just inside the front door significantly reduces my odds of winning the battle of the bulge. It's a good thing I wasn't invited to be a participant in King Nebuchadnezzar's training program with Daniel. I probably would have been the drunk, fat kid waiting tables in the overflow palace dining room.

In his landmark book, *Emotional Intelligence*, Daniel Goleman has some very keen insights about self-control. Goleman builds upon numerous studies in behavioral sciences and neurosciences to show that there are multiple intelligences exhibited by people. In fact, he debunks the once widely held position that cognitive intelligence (as measured by IQ tests) is the best predictor of success. Instead, he writes that there is a much more significant ability—emotional intelligence. Emotional intelligence refers to our ability to manage feelings and impulses. It involves being aware of our emotional state as well as the emotions of others, and managing ourselves so that we make good choices. It shows up in how we are able to motivate ourselves, delay gratification, and self-soothe.

Goleman refers to emotional aptitude as "a meta-ability, determining how well we can use whatever other skills we have, including raw intellect."[14] In other words, our ability to control our emotions determines how well we use our other abilities. Imagine the physically gifted athlete who gets kicked off the team because of his inability to control his anger, or the honor roll student from high school who flunks out of college after partying way too much, or the dynamic young minister who is run out of his church because of sexual infidelity.

Self-control is primarily about controlling our emotions. It is about dealing with disappointment and learning to get past it instead of allowing ourselves to sink into depression. It is also about maintaining our balance when we are being congratulated and not getting carried away by the accolades. It is about resisting the excitement of momentary pleasure in order to enjoy the fruit harvested in the right time and right circumstances. Our ability to control our emotions plays a huge part in determining our success—and failure.

Let me allow Daniel Goleman to speak directly to this point. "Emotional self-control— delaying gratification and stifling impulsiveness—underlies accomplishment of every sort. People who have this skill *tend to be more highly productive and effective in whatever they undertake.*"[15] It sounds like he's been reading 2 Peter 1.

Food for Thought

Everyone who competes in the games exercises self-control in all things. They then do it to receive a perishable wreath, but we an imperishable.
—1 Corinthians 9:25, NASB).

Like a city that is broken into and without walls Is a man who has no control over his spirit.
—Proverbs 25:28, NASB

Anyone can become angry—that is easy. But to be angry with the right person, to the right degree, at the right time, for the right purpose, and in the right way—that is not easy.

—Aristotle

To live a disciplined life, and to accept the result of that discipline as the will of God—that is the mark of a man.

—Tom Landry

The command of one's self is the greatest empire a man can aspire unto, and consequently, to be subject to our own passions is the most grievous slavery. He who best governs himself is best fitted to govern others. He who reigns within himself and rules his passions, desires and fears is more than a king.

—John Milton

CHAPTER 6

PERSEVERANCE—"STICK TO IT"

I love the movie *Rudy*. It's based on the true story of a young man who dreamed of playing college football for the fabled Notre Dame "Fighting Irish." Rudy Ruettiger was a marginal student and scrappy-but-undersized football player at Joliet Catholic High School as a teenager. After graduating, he applied to become a student at the University of Notre Dame but was rejected. He then spent two years in the US Navy and two more years working in a power plant, but still held onto his dream of playing for coach Ara Parseghian at Notre Dame. In order to get close to the school, he applied and was admitted to Holy Cross College, which was also in South Bend, Indiana.

In the movie, Rudy pretends to be a student at Notre Dame, even as he struggles academically at the less-rigorous Holy Cross. He discovers that he suffers from dyslexia, which makes it tough to keep up in class. But he gets help from tutors and learns to compensate for his condition. His grades improve and eventually he is admitted to Notre Dame—on the fourth try.

Still, Rudy didn't just dream of attending Notre Dame or even just graduating from there. He intended to play for the powerhouse football program. Fortunately for him, the Irish allowed students to work with the team as walk-ons, and Rudy soon became a scout team member. Unfortunately, the scout team members were nothing more than live tackling dummies for the real players.

Rudy endured two seasons of brutal practices, being hit and humiliated by the much bigger Irish varsity players. And even though he was technically on the team, he wasn't allowed to suit up for the actual games—only practices. While other scout team members let their dreams die and quit the team, Rudy kept coming back. Not only that, he became almost like a team mascot. But he didn't want to be a mascot—he wanted to play.

Finally, in the last regular season game of his last year, Rudy was allowed to not only suit up for the game, he got to play for three snaps at the end of the game. And on the last play, he even sacked the quarterback. Rudy not only played for the University of Notre Dame Fighting Irish, according to legend, he was the first player in school history to be carried off the field at the end of the game.

Rudy Ruettiger is the poster child for perseverance.

Perseverance is the characteristic of persisting or remaining constant to a purpose, idea, or task in spite of obstacles. In some English Bible translations, such as the King James Version, the word that is used in 2 Peter 1:6 is *patience*. Perseverance carries two connotations. One is to continue to do something even when it becomes hard to do. This is what Paul is urging us to use when he says, "Let us not be weary in well-doing, for in due season we shall reap, if we faint not" (Galatians 6:9, KJV). The other connotation is to wait on something that (or someone who) you believe is coming. This is the idea that we as Christians hold dear when we speak of waiting for the return of the Lord Jesus Christ.

Christ Himself clearly exhibits patience/perseverance with all of us throughout our lives. I cannot be alone in marveling at the fact that God has not struck me down for some of the things I've done. The Apostle Paul is a witness as well. In his first letter to his young apprentice, Timothy, Paul expresses his own gratitude that Christ stuck with him through his past misdeeds. In fact, Paul says of himself that, before Christ appointed him an apostle, he was "a blasphemer and a persecutor and a violent man" (1 Timothy 1:13).

Luke gives the details to back up Paul's story. In the book of Acts, Luke records that Paul, who was then called Saul, was one of the Jewish officials who gave the approval to have Stephen stoned to death for being a disciple of Christ. Later, Paul decided to lead the spread of the persecution of Christ's disciples to Damascus. Paul went to Damascus with letters from the Jewish High Priest authorizing him to arrest any Christians there and bring them to Jerusalem for trial. But on his way to Damascus, the risen Jesus personally intervened and turned his life around (Acts 9).

Years later, Paul has come to an understanding of why Christ has chosen to use him in such a powerful way. He tells Timothy, "…so that in me, the worst of sinners, Christ Jesus might display His *unlimited patience* as an example for those who would believe on Him and receive eternal life" (1 Timothy 1:16). No matter how bad we are, Christ never gives up on us. That's perseverance.

The importance of perseverance to becoming an effective, productive Christian applies in both senses of the word. In our Christian walk, we experience both strong opposition and times of unfruitfulness. There are times when keeping the faith, being virtuous, and especially controlling our flesh, is especially challenging.

For example, many Christians have experienced situations in church that made it tough to press forward. Perhaps it involves the moral failure of a church leader who we have trusted and followed. In those times, we feel betrayed, angry, and deeply disappointed. It is tempting to simply walk away from that church and refuse to be associated with any other local body of believers. We can even justify this on the grounds that we don't see anything in the Bible about church membership. If it sounds like I've been through this before—you're right. But the truth is, the church was God's idea.

Jesus Christ established it and promised to lead it to victory over evil (Matthew 16:18).[16] He also said that the unity of Christians would be a testimony to the world that He is from God (John 17:20–21).[17] But sometimes it takes perseverance to maintain unity with the local church.

Patience (perseverance through waiting) is most glaringly necessary when it comes to prayer. Prayer, as I mentioned before, is one of the most important ways that we exercise our faith. We pray to God because we believe in Him and we believe that He rewards those who diligently seek Him (Hebrews 11:6). We believe God's word when it says if we ask God for something he'll give it to us (John 15:7).

But let's be honest. We've probably all asked God for something and haven't gotten it—yet. I can still hear an old refrain that the saints used to say when I was a kid. "He may not come when you want Him, but He's always on time." It seems to me that *wait* is the most common answer to prayer. If you are going to ask God for something, you'd better have some perseverance.

Another reason that perseverance is necessary is because of the nature of God's work. We want to be effective, productive Christians. That implies that we want to work with God to accomplish what He is doing in our lives. We must realize then that God often works through processes, and processes take time. We prefer quick results, but God doesn't always do things in one or two quick steps.

Just think of the human body that God designed. We begin as an embryo, nurtured in a womb. It takes, on average, nine months for the embryo to become a fetus who is prepared to enter the world. During this time, the fetus is fed vital nutrients through a cord that attaches them to the mother. Then, once the baby is born, it grows. Over eighteen years, it goes from a mostly helpless little bundle of less than ten pounds (usually) to a walking, talking, young adult weighing well over a hundred pounds.

And that's just physical maturity. Emotional maturity takes much longer. Unfortunately, some people never achieve it. I'm willing to bet that God can produce a perfectly mature human being in an instant if He so chooses. In fact, most people believe he did just that when He created Adam. But the rest of us must go through the growth process. Even Jesus had to go through it. Most of what God does, He does through processes. It takes perseverance and patience to stick with Him.

Because God created the world, the universal application of perseverance is rather obvious. Much of the world works through processes. It takes time and steps to accomplish most things. And most of the time, when you are trying to accomplish anything of worth, there will be obstacles and opposition that must be overcome. So not only do you have to be about it, believe you can do it, do it right, understand it, and control yourself, you must also stick to it. Through difficulties and over obstacles, you have to stick to it. This is particularly true when it comes to earning a college degree.

I was thirty-five years old when I graduated from college with a bachelor's degree in Organization Management. By that time, I'd attended three different colleges and had three different majors. Along the way, I'd fathered four children, gotten married, and had changed jobs six times. I earned the degree attending an accelerated degree completion program at Calumet College of St. Joseph while working full-time as a service representative in a call center.

At one point, when I initially started the program, I became discouraged because of the fast pace and the workload. But I had a friend at work, Sharon, who was working on her Ph.D. in education. I'll never forget what she told me one day after I told her I was considering quitting the degree program.

She encouraged me to stick to it and offered an explanation for why the pace and workload seemed so hard. She said, "earning a degree is a test of your tenacity." I knew that I was intelligent enough to earn the degree. But I had to face the question of whether I was tough enough. I had to develop perseverance.

Food for Thought

Let us not lose heart in doing good, for in due time we will reap if we do not grow weary.

—Galatians 6:9, NASB

Therefore, do not throw away your confidence, which has a great reward. For you have need of endurance, so that when you have done the will of God, you may receive what was promised.

—Hebrews 10:35–36, NASB

By perseverance, the snail reached the ark.

—Anonymous

Therefore be patient, brethren, until the coming of the Lord. The farmer waits for the precious produce of the soil, being patient about it, until it gets the early and late rains.

—James 5:7, NASB

Consider it all joy, my brethren, when you encounter various trials, knowing that the testing of your faith produces endurance. And let endurance have its perfect result, so that you may be perfect and complete, lacking in nothing.

—James 1:2–4, NASB

Water wears away stone.

—Job 14:19

Chapter 7

GODLINESS—"FEAR GOD"

There is an interesting story told in the book of 1 Samuel that says a lot about how we sometimes treat God. The story concerns the Israelite nation before the time of the kings but after their miraculous deliverance from Egypt and entrance into the promised land. During this time, the Israelites had a running feud with the Philistines. The Philistines were a pagan nation that existed within the borders of the promised land. The wars with the Philistines were an extension of Israel's campaign to defeat all foreigners within their territory.

In 1 Samuel chapters 4 through 6, we read of a fascinating period of the wars. It begins unremarkably, with the Israelites squaring off against the Philistines one day. Unfortunately, the Israelites were roundly defeated, losing about 4,000 men in the battle. When the surviving army met with the elders of Israel, they concluded that they had not been religious enough to win the battle. The plan they hatched is where it really gets interesting.

They sent for the Ark of the Covenant and the priests to accompany them into the next battle. When the priests showed up in the camp with the Ark, everyone let out such a loud cheer that the earth shook. The army was now all fired up to go to battle and defeat the enemy. However, there were two problems that they hadn't anticipated.

First, this also motivated the Philistines to fight even harder. Second, and more importantly, the Ark of the Covenant was not a good-luck charm. The Ark of the Covenant was a mobile monument, made at the specific and detailed direction of God. It was meant to represent the presence of God. It was the center of their sacrificial system of worship.

However, the priests, who were responsible for administering the elaborate system of sacrifices, had not been exhibiting the proper respect for God while completing their duties. In fact, the priests were stealing the sacrifices for themselves instead of offering them all. The priests were even using their office to seduce the women who came to bring their offerings into having sex with them.

Despite being led into battle by the symbols of God's presence, the Israelites were beaten even worse. This time thirty thousand of their soldiers were killed. And to add insult to injury, the Philistines captured the Ark of the Covenant and killed the two dirty priests who brought it. But God wanted to make sure everyone knew that it was not His power that failed that day.

The Philistines carried the Ark to their city and placed it in the temple of one of their pagan gods, Dagon. Dagon was represented by a statue with the body of a fish and the head and hands of a man. After the Ark was placed next to the statue of Dagon overnight, something strange happened. When the temple handlers came back the next morning, the Dagon statue had somehow fallen on its face and was lying in front of the Ark. The Philistines probably thought that was strange, but they reset the Dagon statue back on its pedestal and carried on.

The very next morning, when the Philistines opened the temple again, they were horrified at the sight. Dagon was now lying on the floor in front of the Ark again, but the head and hands of the statue had been severed. A short time later, the people of that city began to be smitten with tumors. In a panic, they called the Philistines from other cities to meet and discuss what to do. When the rest came, they too began to break out in tumors. The land was also hit with a huge infestation of mice.

They tried sending the Ark to another city, Ekron, but the people there said, "Oh, no you don't. We don't want it!" So the Philistines put the Ark on a cart, added a box of little gold icons (made to look like tumors and mice), hitched it all to a couple of cows, pointed it toward one of the Israelite cities, and sent it all back. The Philistines learned the hard way what the people of Israel had forgotten—that the God of Israel is not to be trifled with.

Godliness is a term that you don't hear much outside of a seminary classroom or stained-glass cathedral. The term sounds like it should mean to be like God. But it doesn't. Godliness means respect or reverence of God. Reverence is what people used to have when, as they walked past a church, they would straighten up, lower their voices, and stop cursing.

Respect for God is what used to keep thieves, who robbed stores, homes and pedestrians, from stealing from churches. Godliness may even be exemplified when someone says, "Excuse me, Reverend" when they use the Lord's name in vain in the presence of a preacher. All these things are displays of godliness—when they are sincere. They exhibit a respect for God, even if the person is short on obedience to God.

But, as the story above illustrates, displays of godliness are false when they are merely symbolic. It is not true godliness when it doesn't emanate from a sincere respect—even fear—of God. Godliness is not wearing a cross in the hope that people will think you are a good person. It is not going to church in hopes that it will change your luck. It is not bowing your head and pointing your right hand to the sky, while gently tapping your left fist to your chest after scoring a touchdown, because your play-cousin passed away last week.

True godliness is a deep and abiding awareness that God deserves all glory, praise, and honor for everything good that we do. It is also a deep and abiding knowledge that He is not to be trifled with.

The thing that makes godliness so necessary for becoming an effective, productive Christian is its impact on our motivations. Being a Christian means putting your faith and trust in Jesus Christ as the son of God and savior, and accepting Him as Lord of your life. That last part is where we have a tendency to trail off. Accepting Jesus as Lord is an integral part of salvation.

Paul makes it clear in his letter to the Romans, writing concerning the salvation of Jewish people. He says, "that if you confess with your mouth *Jesus as Lord*, and believe in your heart that God raised Him from the dead, you shall be saved" (Romans 10:9). The confession Paul speaks of here is not just a formality. Its significance is rooted in the meaning of the term *Lord*.

The Jews, as we do today, used the term *Lord* to refer to God. On the other hand, the word was used in the Greek and Roman world as a title to indicate someone who had great authority. Remember, Paul was writing to Roman Christians. In either case, the term was used to refer to someone to whom you had to submit. In some cases, the Romans were said to indicate their allegiance to the emperor as a god by proclaiming, "Caesar is Lord."

The Jews of that era objected to the use of the title in reference to the Roman emperor because of the religious connotation. So when Paul advises the Roman Christians that the confession that should be made for salvation is the phrase "Jesus is Lord," he is saying that salvation involves submission to Christ. I've said all that to explain this. Our quest to become effective, productive Christians cannot be a mere tactic or program to achieve the life that we want. Our relationship with God should not be cultivated for the purpose of getting what we want. This is, at best, a misunderstanding of who God is. At worse it is disrespectful to God.

We must relate to God as Lord and master of our lives. He is the supreme authority and requires us to submit to His will. This is not to say that being an effective, productive Christian does not benefit us in many ways. But the ultimate respect for God is to accept that He has a plan for our lives and seek to discover and live out that plan.

Aside from the religious context, the concept behind godliness is respect for authority. God is the ultimate authority and, according to Paul, all other authority is derived from Him (Romans 13:1). It is important, then, for us to respect those who are in authority. This includes civil authorities, such as police and government officials, as well as those in authority over us in other capacities. In order to be successful in our jobs and careers, we have to have a healthy respect for those in leadership above us. In the corporate world and other organizations, the new buzzword for this is *alignment*, as in "we must be properly aligned."

This is not merely a superficial notion where we dress up when the CEO will be visiting our office, or we stand when the president enters the room. In an organization, in order for things to work, people throughout that organization must pull in the same direction. Those in authority set that direction. When people lose respect for those in authority, things break down. It affects the ability of the organization to accomplish its purpose.

This is illustrated in one of my all-time favorites movies. In the 1997 classic *A Few Good Men*, Jack Nicholson explains this with characteristic clarity as Marine Col. Nathan Jessup. He portrays the commander of the Marine base in Guantanamo Bay, Cuba, where Marine Private Santiago dies at the hands of two of his platoon mates. Tom Cruise plays their defense attorney, the young, brash, Lt. Caffey.

The highlight of the trial occurs when Lt. Caffey calls Col. Jessup to testify, with the intent of coaxing him into confessing that he gave the order to his underlings to deliver a midnight beating (called a "Code Red") to Private Santiago. Unfortunately, the illegal discipline proved fatal and the two Marines are on trial for murder. No one in the chain of command will admit to ordering the Code Red. In fact, Col. Jessup testified that he ordered his men not to touch Private Santiago. But Lt. Caffey and his crack legal team uncover a critical flaw in their denials.

At this point, Caffey asks Col. Jessup if there's any chance that his subordinates ignored or forgot his alleged order that Santiago was not to be touched. With his trademark intensity, Nicholson, as Col. Jessup, attempts to turn the tables on his inquisitor with a barrage of his own questions.

"You ever serve in an infantry unit, son?"

"No," replies Caffey.

"Ever serve in a forward area?"

"No."

"Ever put your life in another man's hands, ask him to put his life in yours?"

"No," replies Caffey again.

At this, Jessup delivers his point with words, curled lips, and a steely glare. "We follow orders, son. We follow orders, or people die! It's that simple!"

I'm certainly not advocating blind allegiance to every order given by a person in authority. In fact, Col. Jessup was lying about having given an order not to touch Private Santiago. Later in the climactic scene, he admits to ordering the Code Red and is placed under arrest.

But Jessup's statement is nonetheless true. In fact, he had given the order to deliver the discipline, and those underneath him followed through with brutal efficiency. Those in authority have a greater responsibility, and therefore greater accountability. We may respectfully ask questions or even push back if we have valid reservations about direction being given from above. But, at the end of the day, we must either respect those in authority and follow them, or conclude that they are not worthy of that respect, and quit following them.

Food for Thought

But godliness with contentment is great gain.

—1 Timothy 6:6, NIV 2011

For physical training is of some value, but godliness has value for all things, holding promise for both the present life and the life to come.

—1 Timothy 4:8, NIV 2011

Let everyone be subject to the governing authorities, for there is no authority except that which God has established. The authorities that exist have been established by God. Consequently, whoever rebels against the authority is rebelling against what God has instituted, and those who do so will bring judgment on themselves.

—Romans 13:1–2, NIV 2011

The fear of the Lord is the beginning of knowledge.

—Proverbs 1:7

There are two kinds of people: those who say to God, "Thy will be done," and those to whom God says, "All right, then, have it your way."

—C. S. Lewis

Heaven is above all yet; there sits a judge that no king can corrupt.

—William Shakespeare in *Henry VIII*

I have lived, sir, a long time. And the longer I live, the more convincing proofs I see of this truth—that God governs in the affairs of men. And if a sparrow cannot fall on the ground without his notice, is it probable that an empire can rise without his aid?

—Benjamin Franklin

Sir, my concern is not whether God is on our side; my great concern is to be on God's side, for God is always right.

—Abraham Lincoln

Chapter 8

BROTHERLY KINDNESS—"BE NICE"

Another of my favorite stories in the Bible is found in 1 Kings 18, which details the showdown on Mt. Carmel between the prophet Elijah, the four hundred and fifty prophets of Baal, and the four hundred prophets of Asherah. It features a display of confidence followed by a stunning display of power, which is then followed by a gruesome display of brutality.

Elijah challenges these rival prophets to a contest to show the wicked Israeli King Ahab that God is all-powerful while their gods, Baal and Asherah, were powerless. It was a showdown of the gods! The pagan prophets set up an altar with wood, laid an ox on it, and pleaded with their gods to rain down fire upon the altar. After Ahab's prophets pleaded with their gods for several hours, to no avail, it was Elijah's turn.

He built an altar with twelve stones, dug a ditch around it, cut up an ox, and then poured water on the whole thing. The ox was soaking wet. The ditch was filled with water. Then Elijah prayed to his God. God responded immediately by sending a blast of fire from heaven that burned up the wet ox, the damp wood, the stones, and even the water in the ditch!

Next, Elijah had all the eight hundred and fifty losers rounded up, and he killed them all. But if that wasn't enough for one day, Elijah, after praying for the end of a three-year drought, outran Ahab back to the capital city. Ahab was in a chariot and Elijah was on foot! And it was pouring rain!!

Unfortunately, Elijah's remarkable spiritual and athletic accomplishments must have left him emotionally drained. When King Ahab got back to the palace and told his wife, Queen Jezebel, what had happened, she issued a decree that essentially put out a hit on Elijah. After having done all that he'd done that day, including killing eight hundred and fifty men, Elijah became afraid and ran for his life.

A month and a half later, we find Elijah sitting alone in a cave—hiding! When the Lord asks him what's up, we discover a clue as to why Elijah has all of a sudden lost his courage. Elijah replies (and I paraphrase), "I have been zealous for you, but your people have broken their covenant with you and killed your prophets. *I am the only one left.*" Elijah felt like he had been doing it all by himself. After showing him more displays of His power, the Lord let Elijah in on something. There were seven thousand Hebrews who hadn't worshipped the false gods, including one hundred and fifty other prophets who had been hiding in caves. Elijah was not alone.

Like many of us today, Elijah had been toiling under the misconception that he had to do it all alone. Thus far, the qualities we have covered seem to underscore the point that this is an individual journey. It is about *my* diligence, *my* faith, *my* virtue, and so on. There is a risk of becoming so isolated in pursuing our goals that we burn out or become discouraged. As the story of Elijah demonstrates, even when we are achieving great successes on our own, we need to know that there are others on this journey with us. And how we interact with these others makes a difference in whether we ultimately reach our goal.

The next principle that Peter tells us to add is brotherly kindness. In some Bible translations, it is also known as *brotherly love* or *mutual affection*. This principle has to do with how we treat and interact with others. However, when Peter lists this in his letter, he is describing a quality that we should develop within ourselves. It is a quality that we should consistently use when interacting with others.

Although the term might seem to refer to interaction with family or those close to us, it is broader than that. At the very least, the context in which the word is used in scripture shows that we should extend it to all Christians. Wisdom dictates that brotherly kindness be spread to all unless there is some substantial reason not to.

In practice, brotherly kindness can be reduced to the simple command—be nice. This is in contrast to what seems like the prevalent attitude of our times. From political discourse, to reality television, to social media, there is no shortage of mean-spirited communication in our society. We don't even have to consider some of the pure hatred, racism, and terrorism exhibited by those who cannot seem to shake these evils from their consciousness.

Even normal people too often slip into patterns of behavior that are, at best, inconsiderate and, at worst, cruel. And, by the way, when you defend yourself from criticism that you callously hurt someone with your words by saying, "but it was true," it doesn't make the person feel any better. In fact, that's like pouring salt in the wound.

The need for brotherly kindness is indirectly illustrated by the story about Elijah above. As the depressed prophet stood before God in the cave, he was given instructions on what to do next. God told him to anoint a new king, Hazael, in the country of Aram, and then anoint a new king in Israel, Jehu. Next, he was to anoint his own successor as prophet, Elisha. These men would finish the task of ridding the kingdom of those who were opposed to the God of Israel. God's message seemed to be, "You can't do this by yourself." And that goes for us today too—we can't do it by ourselves. We need the cooperation of others.

In particular, when it comes to becoming like Christ, we must understand that God instituted the church as one of the primary vehicles—along with the family—through which we are to be perfected. In his letter to the Ephesians, Paul wrote that leadership gifts were given to equip Christians to do the work of ministry so that the body of Christ is edified (Ephesians 4:11–12). The "body of Christ" is an oft-used reference in the Bible for the church.

Also, most of Paul's letters were written to churches. In those letters, one of his recurring themes is unity among believers. Maintaining unity requires that we treat each other with respect and kindness. This is proven often when we see people leave their church because of how they were treated by someone there. In those cases, it is easy to attribute the split to the person's immaturity. Most of the time that is an accurate analysis. However, the accuracy of our analysis doesn't diminish the damage it does to the unity of the church. Sometimes the damage can be avoided by simply being nice.

Jesus Himself also prayed that Christians be unified. In fact, Jesus made it clear that our unity will show the world that He was sent by God (John 17:23). He also said that the credibility of our claim to be followers of Christ is affected by how we treat each other (John 13:34). Imagine what people think when they see Christians being unkind to each other. Imagine what they feel when they experience Christians being unkind to them. It is a reflection of Christ—a bad one.

The universal application of brotherly kindness pertains to relationships in every area of our lives. In our personal lives, kindness goes a long way toward building friendships, both romantic and platonic. No one likes hanging around someone who is mean or inconsiderate. In business and careers, we do ourselves a disservice when we neglect the simple lesson that we learned in kindergarten—be nice.

We all recognize that in order to get most things done at work, we need the support of those we work with. And if we have any desire to advance in our careers, we know we need others to promote us—or at least to not oppose our promotion. Although it may seem unfair at times, people want to work with other people that they like. They usually don't look for opportunities to help a person who regularly ticks them off. One obvious way to build and maintain a relationship with someone is to be nice to them.

This is the central theme for one of the most popular books ever written. This book, originally written in 1936, has sold over 15 million copies. It is the basis of a training seminar taken by billionaire investor Warren Buffett at twenty years old, for which he still has the completion certificate hanging on his wall. Many consider it one of the most impactful self-help books written in the twentieth century. It is called *How to Win Friends and Influence People*, written by Dale Carnegie. In it, Carnegie offers some simple principles for dealing with people that are time-honored. His advice includes: become genuinely interested in other people, give honest and sincere appreciation, and don't criticize, condemn, or complain.

My favorite suggestion from Carnegie is his easiest. It is a tactic that I have learned makes others feel better and also positively affects my own mood. When babies do it, our hearts melt. And doing this more often will positively change the atmosphere around us. Sometimes, all we have to do to show brotherly kindness is—smile.

Food for Thought

Be devoted to one another in brotherly love; give preference to one another in honor.

—Romans 12:10, NASB

Now that you have purified yourselves by obeying the truth so that you have sincere love for each other, love one another deeply, from the heart.

—1 Peter 1:22, NIV 2011

Now about your love for one another we do not need to write to you, for you yourselves have been taught by God to love each other.

—1 Thessalonians 4:9, NIV 2011

A faithful friend is the medicine of life.

—Apocrypha, Ecclesiasticus 6:16

The only way to have a friend is to be one.

—Ralph Waldo Emerson

A gentle answer turns away wrath, but a harsh word stirs up anger.

—Proverbs 15:1

CHAPTER 9

LOVE—"THE GOLDEN RULE"

We often hear about haters and people deeming others as haters. But what is a hater? I'm not sure if there is an official definition, so I will take a stab at creating my own. A hater is someone who wants someone else to fail, or do badly. Perhaps they want them to fail out of pure jealousy. Perhaps it's because the person did something bad to them and they want them to receive their comeuppance. Whatever the reason, haters want the object of their hate to do badly. And while the Bible speaks a lot about love, even in scripture there are examples of haters.

The story of Jonah is about more than a guy and a whale. Jonah was a hater. When God ordered him to go warn the Assyrians in Nineveh that God would judge their wickedness, Jonah refused. He knew that if they heed the warning and turn to God, He would forgive them. The Assyrians were their enemies. Jonah had probably been praying every day for God to destroy them.

So instead of warning them, Jonah took the next boat out of town, in the other direction. God had mercy on Jonah. He sent a storm, and then when Jonah was thrown overboard, the big fish sent by God scooped him up and deposited him back on shore three days later.

At this point, Jonah gets the message and goes to Nineveh and tells them what God said. And just as Jonah feared, they heard the warning and turned their hearts toward God. This made Jonah angry with God and he threw a little hissy fit. Jonah went and sat outside the city, sulking and praying to God to die. Even after God gave him another object lesson in grace, Jonah still had an attitude. Jonah was a hater.

His story is a cautionary tale. God wanted Jonah to exemplify what Jesus would teach later when He said, "Love your enemies, and pray for those who persecute you" (Matt. 5:44). God, on the other hand, was exemplifying love toward the Ninevites, even though they did not worship Him.

Peter encourages us to add love to our brotherly kindness. It is relatively easy to distinguish between love and hate, but in making that distinction, we may be thinking about brotherly kindness rather than love. We may settle for being nice to others rather than progressing to showing love—real love.

Real love is a radical concept. It is something that people have learned to profess—"I love you, brother"—but often don't quite understand. The truth is, we often mistake love for brotherly kindness. In that way, we may develop our people skills well enough that we are caught being nice to people that we wouldn't have been nice to at one point in our lives. We then identify that as love. As mentioned in the last chapter, brotherly kindness is even translated as brotherly love in some versions of the Bible. But real love goes beyond being nice. Real love is more than being affectionate. Real love is radical because it requires sacrifice. Real love is the ultimate, according to Jesus.

One day, a religious man asked Jesus one of those questions that religious people like to ask. He asked Him, "Which is the first commandment of all?"

Jesus answered him, "The first of all the commandments is 'Hear, O Israel, the Lord our God, the Lord is one. And you shall love the Lord your God with all your heart, with all your soul, with all your mind, and with all your strength.' This is the first commandment. And the second like it is this—'You shall love your neighbor as yourself.' There is no other commandment greater than these."

So the scribe said to Him, "Well said, Teacher. You have spoken the truth, for there is one God, and there is no other but He. And to love Him with all the heart, with all the understanding, with all the soul, and with all the strength, and to love one's neighbor as oneself, is more than all the whole burnt offerings and sacrifices."

Now, when Jesus saw that he answered wisely, He said to him, "You are not far from the kingdom of God" (Mark 12:28–34). I think what Jesus was saying to this man was— now that you understand how important love is, you are not far, but to get all the way, you must do it.

An example of the difference between brotherly kindness and love can be seen in the relationship between Abraham and his nephew Lot. In Genesis 13, Abraham has been blessed greatly by God and has accumulated a lot of stuff, including servants and livestock. His nephew, who lived with him, had also accumulated stuff. One day

Abraham decided that they needed to split up so that they could have more room.

Abraham went to Lot and pitched the idea. In a magnanimous gesture, Abraham told him, "If you go take the left, then I will go to the right, or, if you go to the right, then I will go to the left" (Genesis 13:9). Abraham was being nice. Since Abraham was the older of the two and the uncle, he could have chosen the land he wanted first, but instead he allowed Lot to choose the best of the land and Abraham took what was left.

Later, Abraham found out that his nephew had been taken captive by an army that had defeated the people who lived around the city that Lot had chosen. Now, Abraham could have said, "Well, it serves him right. Since he chose those cities, now he has to deal with it." But this is where he exemplifies love. Abraham sacrificed himself and his household by gathering his men together and going off to rescue Lot. Abraham risked his own life to save his nephew. That's love.

Love is more than simply affection or kindness. To love someone is to desire to do what's best for him or her. Jesus best explains love in His sermon when He said, "In everything, therefore, treat people the same way you want them to treat you, for this is the Law and the Prophets" (Matt. 7:12).

We all want what's best for ourselves (we may not know what's best for us, but whatever we think it is, we want it!) Often, when we are dealing with others, we are mostly thinking of what is best for us, not them. But this is why sacrifice is a key to true love. To love someone is to consider and do what's best for him or her, even if it costs you something.

If we are serious about being like Jesus Christ (being effective and productive Christians) we must follow His example. We know that Jesus, at the end of His earthly days, allowed Himself to be tortured and executed on our behalf. He made the ultimate sacrifice. But, contrary to what we hear from some pulpits these days, his sacrifice was not a one-time—or even two-time—event. He sacrificed his position in heaven to come to earth in a human body.

Consider his response to the temptation of the enemy in the wilderness. At one point, Satan offers to give Him all the kingdoms of the world. Now, obviously, Jesus knew that He would conquer all of the earth eventually. Satan was in a sense saying, "I won't even put up a fight. I know you are God. So I'll just hand over all this to you." But Jesus sacrificed a quick half-victory (Satan would not have been defeated) for a full victory.

Another example of this, told by John (John 12:9–32), is Jesus' response to a request for a meeting. The incident occurred during the high point of Jesus' public ministry. He had just entered Jerusalem at the beginning of the Passover week and received rock-star treatment.

Many Jews from faraway places had traveled to Jerusalem for the religious festivities. The word had spread about Jesus' miracle of raising Lazarus from the dead, and the crowds were coming out to see him. The Jewish officials were filled with jealousy, saying, "See! The world is coming after him." And they were right.

That day, some Greeks approached His disciples and asked for a meeting. Now, the Greeks were the cultural elite of that day.

Alexander the Great had spread classical Greek influence throughout much of the known world, and the Romans had solidified it. So getting the Greeks, with their schools of philosophy, to endorse him would have spread his message and influence throughout the world. In modern times, this would be like having Oprah endorse this book for her book club (wink, wink) or having your business advertised in a Super Bowl commercial. The Greeks could have taken Jesus' brand to the next level. But Jesus sacrificed instant, easy fame and turned down the meeting. He had no time for schmoozing. In a few days, he was going to be executed for our sakes.

Love, as a motivating part of our character, is necessary because it is the reason we are here on earth. We are here to sacrifice on behalf of others. When we do that, we are enriched and exalted. When we make others better, we make the world around us better. It is necessary because being nice isn't enough.

Being diligent, faithful, virtuous, smart, disciplined, tough, and respectful only qualifies us to fulfill the purpose for which God has put us here. Being a great person doesn't mean we are doing great things. To paraphrase Jesus—the greatest things to do are to love God completely, and love others sincerely.

I don't mind admitting it—I get choked up when I watch sports movies. I am particularly moved by the movies that spotlight some ragtag underdog team that comes together to become a winner. These movies usually show individuals struggling with their deficiencies and selfish agendas. I have literally cried while watching movies like *Remember the Titans, Coach Carter,* and even *The Replacements.* These movies feature a collection of damaged individuals that come to form a formidable team under the wise-but-demanding leadership of their coach.

One such movie is *Friday Night Lights*. *Friday Night Lights* is based on the true story of a high school football team in Odessa, Texas. These young men struggle with the extraordinarily high expectations of the town and of their coach, Gary Gaines, who asks them the question, "Can you be perfect?" When their star running back, Boobie Miles, is injured, the challenge is amplified. But they somehow manage to make the playoffs while dealing with the pressures brought on by the adults around them.

Coach Gaines, played by Billy Bob Thornton, balances the need to push his team to excellence with the challenge of handling them as teenagers. His crowning moment is the proverbial pregame locker room speech near the end of the movie. His team, the Permian High Panthers, have made it to the state final against a team that appears bigger, stronger, faster, and meaner.

In his speech, Gaines puts it all in perspective for his young charges. He says, "Being perfect is about being able to look your friends in the eye and know you didn't let them down. I want you to put each other in your hearts forever—because forever is about to happen. Can you live in that moment as best you can, with clear eyes, with love and joy in your heart? If you can do that, then you're perfect."[18]

In sports, business, church, family, or any other endeavor that involves multiple people, love is necessary for lasting success. It is the basis of teamwork. When people on the team are only concerned about themselves, then they will have different agendas. But if they are concerned about each other, and the team as a whole, they are able to accomplish much more.

To use another sports illustration, legendary Coach Phil Jackson, in his book *Eleven Rings: The Soul of Success*, identifies love as *the* critical factor. He says, "It takes a number of critical factors to win an NBA championship, including the right mix of talent, creativity, intelligence, toughness, and of course, luck. But if a team doesn't have the most essential ingredient—love—none of those other factors matter."[19]

Food for Thought

But now faith, hope, love, abide these three; but the greatest of these is love.

—1 Corinthians 13:13

If I speak with the tongues of men and of angels, but do not have love, I have become a noisy gong or a clanging cymbal. If I have the gift of prophecy, and know all mysteries and all knowledge; and if I have all faith, so as to remove mountains, but do not have love, I am nothing. And if I give all my possessions to feed the poor, and if I surrender my body to be burned, but do not have love, it profits me nothing.

—1 Corinthians 13:1–3

A new commandment I give to you, that you love one another, even as I have loved you, that you also love one another. By this all men will know that you are My disciples, if you have love for one another.

—John 13:34–35

Greater love has no one than this, that one lay down his life for his friend.

—John 15:13

CHAPTER 10

GROWTH—"BE BETTER AND BETTER AND BETTER"

We've all been there before—suffering at the mercy of incompetence. Perhaps it's a coworker whose perpetual ineffectiveness creates more work for us. People in customer service jobs have bad days, but now and then, we run across someone who has no clue what they are doing. And who among us hasn't grown irritated at the grocery store while a single cashier labors to check out the very long line of shoppers, but five other clerks stand around like they don't notice it? Some days we seem to be surrounded by ineffective and unproductive people.

Not long ago, my wife and I tried to eat at a restaurant that served chicken and waffles. While I devoured my delicious (and promptly served) breakfast of bacon and eggs, my wife waited impatiently for her chicken and waffles. We watched as two young restaurant employees stood nearby, laughing and chatting. Our loudly cleared throats and vigorous waves did nothing to get their attention.

Finally, after almost completing my meal, I got up, walked over, and asked to speak to the manager. Immediately, one of them half-smiled and said, "I'm the manager." After I expressed my displeasure with how long it was taking to receive my wife's meal, she incorporated the most puzzled look—as if I had asked her if the sun is hot.

She then explained what, to her, seemed like the most obvious thing in the world. "Well, it takes a long time to cook chicken and waffles, sir." Before I could unleash a verbal thrashing, our server walked out of the kitchen with my wife's plate. I followed her back to our table and began to sip my now-cold coffee. And the young manager never noticed my wife's disgust with the piping-hot chicken sitting atop the icy-cold waffles.

In 1969, Laurence Peter and Raymond Hull released a book titled *The Peter Principle* that purported to answer the question of why things always go wrong. In it, they introduced the principle that has been quoted and paraphrased often in the business world. The Peter Principle states: "In a hierarchy, every employee tends to rise to his level of incompetence."[20]

Though the book is very humorous, it is actually "a serious business book disguised as a parody."[21] The authors' real purpose seems to be to warn people about seeking promotion and advancement for its own sake, rather than seeking the "improvement of the quality of experience."[22] They make a strong case for the notion that our thirst for personal advancement and material possessions is a prescription for failure. According to the Peter Principle, people eventually rise to a level that is beyond their capabilities and become incompetent. But according to the Apostle Peter- author of the scriptural letter that gives us what I am calling The Second Peter Principle - it doesn't have to be that way.

In their final chapter, Laurence Peter and Raymond Hull recommend that we seek to improve our quality of life by avoiding life incompetence.[23] While appreciating the point of view of *The Peter Principle*, I think the Bible has a greater principle that kills incompetence—the Second Peter Principle. God guarantees that we will be effective and productive in all we do if we develop Christ-like character. And the tenth quality that supports the Second Peter Principle is the key to overcoming the Peter Principle. This quality prevents people from rising to their level of incompetence. The final quality that the apostle Peter advocates is growth.

The term *growth* means an increase in size, value, or importance. It also refers to the process of maturing. In 2 Peter 1:8, Peter says, "For if you possess these qualities *in increasing measure*, they will keep you from being ineffective and unproductive in your knowledge of our Lord Jesus Christ" (NIV). So, just as the first quality, diligence, refers to how the others should be pursued, this last quality deals with all of the others. In this case, Peter insists that we not only pursue the possession of these qualities, but that we continue to *grow* in them.

The idea of growing is fundamental to our lives, and as such, is a thread that weaves throughout the Bible. In many cases, the concept of growth refers to some material or physical increase. In Genesis 1:28, God's first words directly to man were, "Be fruitful and increase in number." Four times in chapters 2 through 4 of Genesis it is pointed out that man's job was to cultivate the ground—which means to make it grow.

Later, in Genesis 15, God chooses Abraham to start a nation to call His own, and He makes it clear that Abraham will experience prodigious growth in his family and possessions. The story of the descendants of Abraham is told in the rest of the Old Testament as they grow into a great nation even through periods of enslavement, war, and internal dissension. The New Testament is a story of the growth of the church from the miraculous birth, death, and resurrection of Jesus Christ, the foundational work of the apostles, and the evangelistic efforts of Paul and others. The postbiblical history of the church is one marked by explosive growth.

It is easy, and therefore common, to think of growth and increase as it pertains to material things. However, much of the Bible encourages us to pursue spiritual growth. We are encouraged to grow in grace and knowledge of Christ (2 Pet. 3:18); increase our faith (Luke 17:5); increase in love for one another (1 Thess. 3:12); and to grow up in all aspects in Christ (Eph. 4:15). Peter even likens the word of God to pure milk that causes us to "grow in respect to salvation" (1 Pet. 2:2).

The book of Revelation tells of the climactic return of Christ and establishment of a new earth after a period of great tribulation. In the end, what is revealed is a church that has grown into the image of Christ. So the growth that we refer to in this book is spiritual growth.

The reason that growth is so important is because of our condition as it compares to our mission. As Christians, we are called to go make disciples everywhere, baptize these disciples, and teach them what Christ has commanded (Matt. 28:19–20). These were Jesus' words to his disciples just before He left them on earth to carry out the mission.

Later, Paul elaborated on the overall mission when he gave instructions concerning leadership to the church in Ephesus. He said, "And He gave some as apostles, and some as prophets, and some as evangelists, and some as pastors and teachers, for the equipping of the saints for the work of service, to the *building up* of the body of Christ; until we all attain to the unity of the faith, and of the knowledge of the Son of God, *to a mature man*, to the measure of the stature which belongs to the *fullness* of Christ. As a result, *we are no longer to be children*, tossed here and there by waves and carried about by every wind of doctrine, by the trickery of men, by craftiness in deceitful scheming; but speaking the truth in love, *we are to grow up* in all aspects into Him who is the head, even Christ, from whom the whole body, being fitted and held together by what every joint supplies, according to the proper working of each individual part, *causes the growth of the body for the building up of itself* in love" (Ephesians 4:11–16, NIV, emphasis mine).

Let me summarize what Paul says this way; together we are to grow into a body of mature Christians that reflect Christ. Paul points out that we begin as children. Elsewhere in scripture, he says that when we are born again, we become "new creatures" (2 Cor. 5:17). To be born again is to begin a new life as disciples of Christ. A disciple is a student—a person who follows another to learn from them.

As disciples of Christ, we are not simply members of a church, we are on a journey of growth toward maturity into what God wants us to be as individuals and, more importantly, as part of His church. So to disregard our spiritual growth is to refuse to cooperate with God's plan and our own destiny.

Peter tells us unequivocally, "For if you possess these qualities in increasing measure, they will keep you from being ineffective and unproductive in your knowledge of our Lord Jesus Christ." This statement crystallizes the Second Peter Principle. God's plan is centered on us—His people—becoming like Christ. The process of becoming like Christ is the process of growing in these qualities—faith, virtue, knowledge, self-control, perseverance, godliness, kindness, and love. And growth in these qualities requires diligence.

We can all identify milestones in our lives that demonstrate our growth process. We matriculate through the grade levels in education marked by graduations. Children grow physically in height and sometimes mark the progress with scratches on a doorpost. However, growth into adulthood is seen as the major goal. Adulthood is generally understood as the point in which an individual can handle his or her life without dependence on their parents. Once reaching that milestone, most people are not content to just be independent. Most people want to continue to experience more in their lives. Most people want to continue to grow.

Like the rest of the qualities, growth has a universal application that is important for being effective and productive in our lives. In order to be truly effective and productive at anything, we must embrace growth and improvement as a guiding principle. One of the best examples of this is the growth of Japan as a world economic power in the last half of the twentieth century.

In 1945, President Truman made the fateful decision to employ nuclear bombs to end World War II. In August of that year, the Japanese cities of Hiroshima and Nagasaki were destroyed using nuclear bombs. The Japanese government surrendered a week later. Between the nuclear devastation and prior conventional bombings of its cities, Japan exited the war in dire straits. However, after a seven-year period of occupation by US forces, Japan began a climb that led the country to become one of the largest economic powers in the world by the 1980s.

There are several factors that contributed to Japan's economic growth, but one important one is the productivity of its businesses. In 1986, Masaaki Imai wrote a book that introduced to the West a concept that he credited with Japan's remarkable growth. The book is called *Kaizen: The Key to Japan's Success.*

Within forty years after the United States bombed Japan with its nuclear arsenal, it appeared that Japan was on the brink of blanketing the United States with its own arsenal of electronics and automobiles. Cars with the Toyota, Honda, and Nissan nameplates filled the roads. Sony televisions, stereos, and personal electronics entertained Americans. Memories were captured on Canon and Nikon cameras. Children demanded the latest Nintendo or SEGA game systems. American hard-earned dollars were being spent by the millions on Japanese goods because they were not only inexpensive but good quality.

The driving force behind this phenomenon was that Japanese business—as well as the rest of their society—had become devoted to a concept that stressed continuous improvement. According to Imai,

"Kaizen means ongoing improvement involving everyone, including both managers and workers. The Kaizen philosophy assumes that our way of life—be it our working life, our social life, or our home life—deserves to be constantly improved."[24] Chiefly because of their dedication to continuous improvement, Japan has become one of the world's most economically and technologically advanced nations. Their commitment to growth led the Japanese to become effective and productive.

Food for Thought

When I was a child, I used to speak like a child, think like a child, reason like a child; when I became a man, I did away with childish things.

—1 Corinthians 13:11, NASB

And Jesus increased in wisdom and in stature and in favor with God and man.

—Luke 2:52

And he said, "The kingdom of God is as if a man should scatter seed on the ground. He sleeps and rises night and day, and the seed sprouts and grows; he knows not how. The earth produces by itself, first the blade, then the ear, then the full grain in the ear. But when the grain is ripe, at once he puts in the sickle, because the harvest has come."

—Mark 4:26–29

But speaking the truth in love, we are to grow up in all aspects into Him who is the head, even Christ, from whom the whole body, being fitted and held together by what every joint supplies, according to the proper working of each individual part, causes the growth of the body for the building up of itself in love.

—Ephesians 4:15–16

Discipleship matters, because we cannot reach our potential without spiritual growth.

—George Barna

The Christian walk is much like riding a bicycle; we are either moving forward or falling off.

—Robert Tuttle

I don't think God is too interested in our success. He is interested in our maturity.

—Fred Smith

So the greatest issue facing the world today, with all its heartbreaking needs, is whether those who, by profession or culture, are identified as "Christians" will become disciples—students, apprentices, practitioners—of Jesus Christ, steadily learning from him how to live the life of the Kingdom of the Heavens into every corner of human existence.

—Dallas Willard, *The Great Omission*

CHAPTER 11

THE PROMISE

In 2 Peter 1:3–10, the apostle Peter makes a bold statement that makes this one of the most powerful passages of scripture. Peter says that this system of qualities is accompanied by a promise from God. God, through His word, has promised that, if we live by this system we will never stumble and will be effective and productive in our Christian lives. If you believe that God keeps His promises, you have to pay close attention to what Peter says here. God *guarantees* that, if you live by this system, you will be effective and productive in your life. And I am humbled to say that I am a witness to the veracity of God's promise.

How did we ever get anywhere without GPS and mapping software? Today, when I want to drive somewhere and don't know how to get there, I get in my car and either enter the address in my car's navigation system, or I enter it into my phone. Within seconds, I have turn-by-turn directions—with a map and even an electronic voice to tell me exactly where to go. But I'm old enough to remember when it wasn't nearly that simple.

Before the NAV systems and smartphones, we used to go online to MapQuest. But when I first got my driver's license, we did it the old-fashioned way—we asked someone for directions. The key to this method being effective was making sure you asked the right person. You especially had to make sure you didn't ask someone who could never admit to being ignorant of anything. There are probably still some people driving around on a trip they started thirty days ago because someone gave them bad directions. I am ashamed to admit that I've even done it myself.

I recall once, years ago, when I worked in downtown Chicago, someone approached me on the street and asked for directions to some building. I was so flattered that they thought I looked like someone who knew their way around in the Chicago Loop that I answered them. I didn't really know where the building was that they were trying to get to, but that seemed like a minor detail. I said, "It's about three blocks that way." I must have figured that they wouldn't have walked far before they realized I had no clue what I was talking about.

The truth is, I started out my adult life like that. People tried to give me directions—my parents, people at church, teachers, and so on. But although I didn't know what to do, or even where I wanted to go, I acted like I did. It didn't work well, and because of that I had an inauspicious beginning. In high school I was a pretty good student, but I wasn't concerned with applying myself. I was a decent athlete too but not really serious about that either.

The three years after graduation was a blur of bad decisions. I became a teenaged father at seventeen and sired another child at twenty. My older kid's mom and I never married. I spent one year in college, where I kind of played football, but quit after realizing that toiling at a Division III school wasn't likely to lead to the NFL. I had a very short stint in the army—I never completed basic training and schemed my way into a general discharge.

Back home in Gary, my buddies and I spent a lot of time drinking and hanging out. My mom made me get a job as a grocery-store clerk, which helped me at least provide a little financial support for my kids. My grandfather let me earn a little extra cash helping him in his small glass business. At twenty-two years old, I had no plan except try to survive and maybe have a little fun doing it.

It would probably be a great story if the next thing that happened was an epiphany or some Damascus Road experience. It wasn't. What really happened next was I started getting a little better. I started trying a little harder. I started applying myself a little more. I got a better job as a delivery driver at a beer distributor. Then I started seeing my wife, and we got married.

I started getting more serious about my life. At the age of twenty-three, I got married. Things were looking up. I tried harder to get a better job. I landed a job as a meter reader, but a month later, I contracted a blood clot in my leg and landed in the hospital. I was summarily terminated.

I went back to my old job but kept looking for a better one. I tried selling fire extinguishers—there was no flame. I tried selling knock-off perfume—the sleazy sales manager kept reminding us to call it "renditions." After getting chased from O'Hare airport for illegal soliciting, something about it just didn't smell right.

I was trying to do what I was supposed to do, but it just wasn't effective. Even after I landed a job as a call center rep, was laid off, and then landed another call center rep position at the phone company, I wasn't feeling it. I hated the work, and frankly, I wasn't much good at it. My productivity was horrible.

What I now know is that, even back then, my Christian upbringing was kicking in. I hadn't committed my life to Christ yet, but I knew that I wasn't on the right track. And I knew that I would never be on the right track unless I gave my life to Christ. The problem was, I still didn't know how to do that. I grew up in church. I knew, intellectually, how church people were supposed to act, but I also didn't believe that I could actually do that. I wasn't a terrible person, but there was nothing in me that lead me to believe that I could be a real Christian.

Then, one day, I went to church to check out the young, charismatic preacher that had somehow gotten my wife to join his church. My intention was to let him know that my wife was off-limits for the old Baptist-preacher-sleeping-with-the-women-in-the-congregation game. But he messed me up.

He preached the gospel—I mean the real, simple, you-are-a-sinner-Christ-died-for-your sins-then-was-resurrected-believe-it-and-give-your-life-to-Him gospel. I'd probably heard it a hundred times, but I'd never really listened. This time, I did listen. When I stood up and walked to the front of the church, I knew I would never be the same.

Soon after my conversion, I began to study the Bible diligently. With the help of my pastor and some new friends, my faith and knowledge grew. I wanted desperately to do the right thing, so I threw away all of my beloved secular music, stopped drinking, and attended church religiously. But I soon found that this Christian life is neither easy nor simple.

People let me down, and so I let them know about it. I received my "calling" to preach. But church was proving to be something that had to be endured. I was fervent in prayer and "the things of God." I was pretty nice to people who had the same mindset and determination as I did. Anyone else had to either be pulled from the flames of hell, or left alone so as not to pull me in with them.

I left one church because of other's failures, left the next one because I didn't really like it and we moved away, and a third because it was imploding. In each of these three churches, I was a leader and a minister. Only in the third did I begin to understand the concept of being a shepherd, rather than just a preacher or ministry leader.

Even with the challenges of being a good churchman, the rest of my life has gone pretty well. My wife and I had two wonderful daughters, and with my two older children, we have been blessed to build a nice little blended family. My two oldest children are now productive, independent adults with families of their own. My two youngest have earned degrees and are building careers.

I went back to school and, finally, at age thirty-five, I earned my bachelor's degree. At work, I was promoted to manager in the call center, and subsequently promoted two more times within three years. A couple of years ago, I was promoted to Director level and find myself having navigated a solid career in a very large company.

From a rocky beginning, God has lead me, through His word, to a fulfilling life. Things aren't perfect—and I certainly am not perfect. But I can honestly say that I am effective and productive in my life as a father, husband, business leader, friend, and even as a minister. And the key to this is the Second Peter Principle that I've learned from 2 Peter 1:3–8. Through the years that I've been writing this book, I have consistently gone back to these scriptures and found direction and inspiration. I have written portions and then gone back months later and found it to be even more impactful. I've used the principle in the writing process. I've used the principle and the ten qualities as a parent and a husband. I've applied them in my career—I have a graphic on my wall in my office with the ten qualities listed.

Diligence—Faith—Virtue—Knowledge—Self Control—Perseverance—Godliness—Kindness—Love—and Growth.

And God has been faithful in his promise that, as I have grown in these qualities and applied them, He has helped me become effective and productive in every area of my life.

END NOTES

1   Malcolm Gladwell, *Outliers: The Story of Success* (Hachette Book Group, 2008, Kindle Edition), 39–40.

2   Dr. Martin Luther King and Henry David Thoreau, *On the Duty of Civil Disobedience by Thoreau & Letter from Birmingham Jail by King* (Kindle Locations 594–595). Final Arbiter. Kindle edition.

3   Luke 6:19 (KJV): "And the whole multitude sought to touch him: for there went *virtue* out of him, and healed *them* all." (Translated as "power" in NIV and NASB versions).

4   Luke 8:46 (KJV): "And Jesus said, Somebody hath touched me: for I perceive that *virtue* is gone out of me." (Translated as "power" in NIV and NASB versions.)

5   Stephen R. Covey, *The 7 Habits of Highly Effective People* (Rosetta Books, 2004, Electronic Version), 97–98.

6   American Heritage Desk Dictionary, 4th ed., s.v. "know."

7   Ibid., "understand"

8   Ibid., "wisdom"

9   "The Benefits of Higher Education for Individuals and Society,"
    The College Board, published 2005, accessed December 11,
    2012, www.collegeboard.com/prod_downloads/press/cost04/
    EducationPays2004.pdf.

10 Ibid.

11 Thomas L. Friedman and Michael Mandelbaum, *That Used To
    Be Us: How America Fell Behind in the World It Invented and How
    We Can Come Back.* (Farrar, Straus and Giroux, 2011, Kindle
    edition), 152.

12 Ibid.

13 R. Kent Hughes, *Disciplines of a Godly Man* (Crossway
    Books,1991), 77

14 Daniel Goleman, *Emotional Intelligence: Why it Can Matter More
    Than IQ.* (Bantam Books, 1995), 36

15 Ibid., 43.

16 Matthew 16:18 (NASB): "I also say to you that you are Peter, and
    upon this rock I will build My church; and the gates of Hades
    will not overpower it."

17 John 17:20–21 (NASB): "I do not ask on behalf of these alone,
    but for those also who believe in Me through their word; that
    they may all be one; even as You, Father, are in Me and I in You,

that they also may be in Us, so that the world may believe that You sent Me."

18 *Friday Night Lights*. 2000. Universal Pictures. Dialogue accessed 8/2/2013 at: http://movies.yahoo.com/movie/friday-night-lights/.

19 Phil Jackson and Phil Delehanty, *Eleven Rings: The Soul of Success*. (Penguin Group, 2013, Kindle Edition), 4.

20 Laurence Peters and Raymond Hull, *The Peter Principle: Why Things Always Go Wrong*. (Harper Collins Publishers, 2009), 15.

21 Ibid., 19

22 Ibid., 26.

23 Ibid., 153.

24 Masaaki Imai, *Kaizen: The Key to Japan's Competitive Success*. (The Kaizen Institute, Ltd.,1986), 3.

Printed in the United States
By Bookmasters